THE
LAST NOMAD

WILFRED THESIGER THE LAST NOMAD

One Man's Forty Year Adventure in the World's Most Remote Deserts, Mountains and Marshes

E. P. Dutton   New York

To the memory of Guy Moore, MC
District Commissioner, Northern Darfar, 1930-46
who taught me to appreciate the desert, its people
and their ways

sive per Syrtis iter aestuosas
sive facturus per inhospitalem
Caucasum vel quae loca fabulosus
lambit Hydaspes

Où sont les neiges d'antan?

Yet each man kills the thing he loves

First American edition published 1980 by E.P. Dutton,
a Division of Elsevier-Dutton Publishing Co., Inc., New York

First published in England 1979 by William Collins Sons
& Co. Ltd. as *Desert, Marsh and Mountain*

Copyright © 1979 by Wilfred Thesiger

Designed by Trevor Vincent
Maps drawn by Tom Stalker-Miller

For information contact:
E.P. Dutton, 2 Park Avenue, New York, N.Y. 10016

Library of Congress Catalog Card Number: 79-90999

ISBN: 0-525-93077-9

10 9 8 7 6 5 4 3 2 1

Author's Foreword

In this book I have used the name *Abyssinia* instead of *Ethiopia*, for it was by this name that the country was known in the times of which I write, from my childhood to the Abyssinian campaign in the Second World War. I have also used *Persia* instead of the country's modern name *Iran*. Persia calls to mind three thousand years of history, splendid cities, mosques, carpets and miniatures: Iran, industrial development and oilfields.

A word on Arabic terminology seems called for. The *Bedu* are the nomadic camel-owning tribes of the Arabian desert. In English they are generally called *Bedouin*, a double plural which they themselves seldom use. I prefer *Bedu*, and use it here. They generally speak of themselves, but not of townsmen or cultivators, as *al Arab*, and when referring to them I have spoken of *Bedu* or *Arabs* indiscriminately. In Arabic *Bedu* is plural, *Bedui* singular, but for the sake of simplicity I have used *Bedu* for singular as well as plural. So as not to confuse the reader I have done the same with names of the tribes: for instance, the singular of Rashid would be *Rashdi*, and of Awamir *Amari*.

Any transliteration of Arabic names leads to dispute. I have tried to simplify as much as possible and have consequently left out the letter *ain*, usually represented by '. Few Englishmen can pronounce this letter correctly; to most readers the frequent recurrence of this unintelligible ' would be confusing and irritating. For the difficult letter *ghain* I have used the conventional *gh*. Experts say this soft guttural sound is pronounced like the Parisian *r*. This letter occurs in the name of a leading character, bin Ghabaisha.

Many people of many nationalities have been kind to me over the years, entertaining me in their houses before and after my journeys, giving me help and sound advice. In this book I have mentioned only a few; it would have filled columns to mention them all. I can only thank them collectively, but none the less sincerely.

Above all I have to thank the Bedu who accompanied me in Southern Arabia. I came to them, a stranger from a world of which they had never heard, and they gave me the freedom of the Desert and the five most memorable years of my life. I have often felt that I get the credit for journeys where I could not have travelled five miles without their help and guidance. I am also deeply grateful to the Marshmen of Iraq, who accepted me into their homes and allowed me to share their lives, in a land reputed to have once been Eden.

Since I described many of my experiences in the Empty Quarter of Arabia and the Marshes of Iraq as fully as I could in my previous books, *Arabian Sands* and *The Marsh Arabs*, I have drawn on passages from these publications. I would therefore like to thank the publishers, Messrs. Longman – now Allen Lane, the Penguin Press – for their kind permission to quote extensively from these two books.

George Webb has read and re-read the text of this book with meticulous care, has checked and re-checked captions and maps, suggesting many improvements, and has made himself responsible for the punctuation – something I have never properly comprehended. Any thanks from me for the infinite trouble he has taken must be inadequate. He has also compiled the index, helped by Diana Webb.

K. B. Fleming, who for more than thirty years has developed and printed my photographs that now fill sixty volumes, made the prints. I realize how much work this has involved. I cannot thank him sufficiently.

I am also extremely grateful to Gillian Gibbins of Collins who has taken infinite trouble over this book, at all stages of its production, and given me much encouragement.

While writing this account I have consulted the diaries which I kept. This has enabled me to describe with accuracy such details as the shape and colour of the dunes in the Empty Quarter. I have also re-read the letters I wrote to my mother at the end of the journeys; my description of the Bakhtiari migration, for instance, derives from one of these.

I alone know what my mother's understanding and encouragement of my travels meant to me. She had gone with my father to Abyssinia in 1910. To reach Addis Ababa, where he would assume charge of the British Legation, they had to travel for weeks with animal transport through desert and mountains. I was born a few months later. During my mother's ten years' residence in Abyssinia that country retained much of the savage splendour of its barbaric past. Having seen it, she would always understand the urge that drove me on my travels – from which I would happily return to the home she provided, in Radnorshire before the War, afterwards in Chelsea. We also went much abroad together, and made some journeys which, though not worth recording, seemed enterprising enough at her age. At eighty-eight she motored beyond the Anti-Atlas, into the edge of the Sahara.

I have here attempted to describe some of the journeys I have made over the past forty-eight years. There have been others, in the Atlas Mountains of Morocco, the highlands of Abyssinia, and East Africa where I have spent happy years among the Turkana and Samburu. There was no room for those journeys in this book. I have led a hard life: this was from choice. It was also an inexpensive one: this was essential. I would not have had it otherwise, nor asked for more. Looking back, I would happily live these years again, in the context of the past.

W.T. *Maralal, Kenya, March 1979*

Contents

List of Maps

Biographical Summary and List of Principal Travels, 1910–78

1910	June	Born at the British Legation, Addis Ababa.
1910–19		Mainly in Addis Ababa.
1911	February-March	Journey by mule and camel to Diredawa, then by train to Jibuti on the coast; leave in England.
1914		Leave in England.
1916		Rebellion in Abyssinia.
	October	Battle of Sagale.
1917	February	Coronation of the Empress Zauditou.
	December	Leave. Berbera, British Somaliland.
1918	January	Leave. Berbera; Aden; India; Delhi and Jaipur.
	April	Return to Addis Ababa.
1919	May	Back to England.
	September	Started at preparatory school, Sussex.
1919–23		Preparatory school
1924–28		Eton.
1929–33		Magdalen College, Oxford.
1930	June-July	Worked passage as fireman on S.S. *Sorrento* to Constantinople and Constanza.
	October-November	Attached to the Duke of Gloucester's Mission to Abyssinia for the Coronation of Emperor Haile Selassie.
	December	Journey in the Danakil country of Abyssinia.
1931	January	Back at Oxford.
	July	Worked on a trawler off Iceland.
1933	June	Went down from Oxford.
	August-December	To Addis Ababa; journey through the Arussi mountains; exploration of the Awash River and to Bahdu in Danakil country.
1934	February-May	Addis Ababa to Bahdu; exploration of Aussa (Danakil); then through French Somaliland to the coast at Tajura; then to England.
	December	Cairo, Egypt.
1935–40		Mainly in the Anglo-Egyptian Sudan.
1935	January	Sudan Political Service; Kutum, Northern Darfur.
1936	June	Syria and Palestine (on leave).
1937	November	Morocco (on leave). Posted to Western Nuer District, Upper Nile.
1938	August-November	Journey to Tibesti (on leave), in French Equatorial Africa.
1939	July	England (on leave). Returned to Sudan on outbreak of war.
1940	June	With Sudan Defence Force at Galabat, fighting against the Italians.
1941	January-June	With 101 Mission in Gojam, Abyssinia; and with Wingate's Gideon Force, campaign to liberate Abyssinia.
	July-mid 1942	Syrian campaign with Druze Legion at Jebel Druze; then with Special Operations Executive (SOE) in Syria.
1942	June	To Egypt, with SOE.
	December	To Western Desert and Tripolitania with Special Air Service (SAS).
1943	June	To Palestine, with SAS.
1944	February	Dessie, northern Abyssinia, as Political Adviser.

1945–50		A substantial part of each year spent in Arabia.
1945	*February*	Left Abyssinia.
	April-June	Saudi Arabia with Desert Locust Unit.
	July-September	England.
	September	Western Aden Protectorate.
	October	Dhaufar; Salala and Qarra Mountains.
	November-December	Southern edge of the Empty Quarter.
1946	*January-March*	Salala to the Hadhramaut.
	April-July	The Hejaz; the Tihama; the Assir; England.
	October-December	Dhaufar; first crossing of the Empty Quarter.
1947	*January-February*	Return to Salala via Inner Oman.
	March-May	Salala to Mukalla (Hadhramaut).
	May-August	The Hejaz; the Tihama; the Assir; Najran.
	September-October	England. Declined permanent Locust Control appointment in the Hejaz.
	November	Hadhramaut; preparations for second crossing of the Empty Quarter.
	December	Began approach to second crossing, from Shibam.
1948	*January-March*	From Manwakh to Sulaiyil. Thence across to Abu Dhabi, Trucial Coast.
	April-May	Buraimi; Sharja; Dubai; by dhow to Bahrain.
	June-September	England.
	October-December	Dubai; by launch to Abu Dhabi; Buraimi; Liwa oasis.
1949	*January-April*	Journeys through Inner Oman; back to Trucial Coast.
	May	By boat via Kuwait to Bushire (Persia); by road through Persia; thence to Iraqi Kurdistan; to Baghdad; later to England.
	November	Back to Trucial Coast.
1950	*January-April*	Second journey into Inner Oman. Left Trucial Coast, by air from Sharja.
	July-September	Iraqi Kurdistan.
	October	The Marshes of Iraq.
	November	Meshed, in Persia.
1951–58		A substantial part of each year except 1957 spent in the Marshes of Iraq.
1951	*February*	The Marshes.
	May-September	Iraqi Kurdistan.
	October	The Marshes.
1952	*February*	The Marshes.
	July-October	Pakistan; North West Frontier Province; Swat and Chitral.
1953	*February*	The Marshes.
	August-October	Pakistan; Hunza.
1954	*February*	The Marshes.
	August-September	Afghanistan; the Hazarajat.
1955	*February*	The Marshes.
	August	Morocco; the High Atlas.
1956	*February*	The Marshes.
	July-August	Afghanistan; Nuristan.
	September	The Marshes.
1957		Writing *Arabian Sands*.
1958	*January-June*	The Marshes.
1959		Abyssinia; with mules from Addis Ababa to the Kenya border (Moyale) and back.
1960	*February*	Abyssinia; with mules from Addis Ababa to Lake Tana; the Simien Mountains; back to Addis Ababa. Back to England.
	December	Kenya; Nairobi; safari with camels in Northern Province.
1961		Safari on foot in Kenya.
1961–2		Writing *The Marsh Arabs*.
1962		Safari on foot in Kenya. Climbed Mt Kilimanjaro (Tanganyika).

1963		Tanganyika; donkey journey through the Masai country.
1964	*June-December*	Persia. Elburz Mountains; with Bakhtiari migration through Zagros Mountains; Dasht-i-Lut.
1965	*June-September*	Afghanistan; Nuristan and Badakhshan; later by road from Kabul via Balkh and Herat to Meshed (Persia).
1966	*May*	To Addis Ababa: ceremony for 25th anniversary of its liberation.
	June-November	With the Royalist forces in the Yemen. Then to England.
1967	*November*	Again with the Royalists in the Yemen.
1968	*January*	Back to England.
1968–76		Kenya, nine months each year, mainly on safari.
1977	*January-March*	From Kenya, via Ethiopia (Addis Ababa and Danakil country), to revisit the Yemen (Yemen Arab Republic), Oman (Muscat, Inner Oman and Dhaufar) and Abu Dhabi (United Arab Emirates).
	March-June	England; later by air to the Far East.
	July-December	Voyage by ketch: Bali, Kalimantan (Borneo), Sulawesi (Celebes), Sarawak, Brunei; visited Royal Geographical Society expedition to Mt Mulu in Sarawak for two weeks. Then by ketch to Singapore. Later to Malay Peninsula; Kuala Lampur.
1978	*January-March*	India; Delhi; Hyderabad. Began to write *Desert, Marsh and Mountain*.
	March-June	England.
	June-December	Kenya, mainly on safari.

Other Books and articles by Wilfred Thesiger

ARABIAN SANDS Longmans (now Allen Lane, Penguin Press) 1959. Later Penguin paperback.
THE MARSH ARABS Longmans (now Allen Lane, Penguin Press) 1964. Later Penguin paperback.

Articles in the Geographical Journal (*Royal Geographical Society*)
ABYSSINIA: The Awash River and the Aussa Sultanate (Jan. 1935).
SAHARA: A Camel Journey to Tibesti (Dec. 1939).
ARABIA: A New Journey in Southern Arabia (Apr. 1947); A Journey through the Tihama, the 'Asir, and the Hijaz Mountains (Oct.–Dec. 1947), Across the Empty Quarter (Jul. 1948); A Further Journey across the Empty Quarter (Jan.–Jun. 1949); Desert Borderlands of Oman (Dec. 1950).
IRAQ: The Marshmen of Southern Iraq (Sep. 1954).
AFGHANISTAN: The Hazaras of Central Afghanistan (Sep. 1955); A Journey in Nuristan (Dec. 1957).

Obituaries: Bertram Thomas (Mar. 1951); H. St. J. B. Philby (Dec. 1960).

Other Articles:
A COLLECTION OF BIRDS FROM DANAKIL, ABYSSINIA (The Ibis, Oct. 1935).
GALLOPING LION (Sudan Notes and Records, 1939).
THE BADU OF SOUTHERN ARABIA (Royal Central Asian Journal, 1950).
THE MADAN OR MARSH DWELLERS OF SOUTHERN IRAQ (*ibid*., 1954).
MARSH DWELLERS OF SOUTHERN IRAQ (National Geographic Magazine, Feb. 1959).

See also:
THE TIMES Special Articles on Abyssinia 31 Jul.–3 Aug. 1934; on Morocco ('The Mind of the Moor') 21 Dec. 1937; on Yemen 21–22 Dec. 1966.
LISTENER 15 Sep. 1947; 4 Dec. 1947; 10 Nov. 1949.
OBSERVER 6 Jun. 1976 (letter captioned 'Defence of Lawrence').
GEOGRAPHICAL MAGAZINE May, Dec. 1948; Feb., Jul. 1949; Jul. 1954.
ILLUSTRATED LONDON NEWS 19 Feb. 1955; 1 Jan. 1956; 5 Dec. 1959; 31 Dec. 1960; 21 Jan. 1961.

Prologue 1910–45

Abyssinia 1910–19

Abyssinian childhood. Myself (aged three) with my brother Brian (two): holding on to an oryx just shot by my father in the Danakil desert.

For nearly fifty years I have lived among tribal people in remote and sometimes dangerous places, in the deserts of Africa and Arabia, in the swamps of the Upper Nile and the marshes of Iraq, in the mountains of the Karakoram and the Hindu Kush. I was only just in time. Recently I motored through the Danakil country which I had explored in 1934. There was a tarmac road along the Awash river with service stations and restaurants, where convoys of lorries carrying petrol drew up during their long journey from Assab to Addis Ababa. I also returned to the interior of Oman, through which I had passed in 1949 when it was more inaccessible than Tibet: again there were tarmac roads and queues of cars. Years ago I wrote: 'While I was with the Arabs I wished only to live as they lived, and now that I have left them I would gladly think that nothing in their lives was altered by my coming. Regretfully, however, I realise that the maps I made helped others with more material aims to visit and corrupt a people whose spirit once lit the desert like a flame.'

I have sometimes wondered what strange compulsion has driven me from my own land to wander in the deserts of the east, living year after year among alien peoples, often in great hardship, with no thought of material reward. The urge to travel and explore probably originated in my childhood. Certainly it was an unusual childhood.

I was born in 1910, the eldest of four brothers, in one of the mud buildings which initially housed the Legation at Addis Ababa where my father was British Minister. Indistinct recollections of camels and of tents, of a river and men with spears, and one vivid picture of my father shooting an oryx when I was three – these are among my earliest memories. But these early memories of desert travel are almost gone, overlaid by later ones of the Abyssinian highlands, for it was there I lived till I was nearly nine.

The golden broom in the garden, iridescent sunbirds among the flowers, the juniper bushes and red gullies behind the house, our *syce* waiting with the ponies, a camp by a waterfall, the dipping flight of green and chestnut bee-eaters, and the crimson flash of a touraco's wings among the trees – these are a few pictures that spring to mind from scores of others. I remember sitting beside my father in the twilight above a gorge, hoping he would get a shot at a leopard; I remember looking for bloodstains and cartridge cases near a small bridge where there had been a fight; listening to my father as he read to me of big game hunting and ox wagons and Zulus, from *Jock of the Bushveld*, as the sun went down behind Wochercher; watching in shocked disbelief the lance head come out through the shoulder of our favourite *sowar* when he had an accident getting on his horse, his grey face and closed eyes as I sat miserably beside him after my brother Brian had galloped off for help. He had dismounted to show us a bird's nest. I can see again the white-robed priests dancing in line before the Ark of the Covenant to the beat of silver drums, surrounded by other priests in richly coloured robes, holding silver crosses in their hands. Above all I can remember some of the events during the Rebellion of 1916 when Lij Yasu was deposed: watching the armies going forth to fight, a seemingly chaotic flood of warriors, mounted and on foot; jostling women driving mules and donkeys laden with pots and sacks of grain; all moving inexorably northward; overhearing the news that Ras Lul Seged's army had been wiped out and that Negus Michael, Lij Yasu's father and king of the north, was advancing on Addis Ababa; seeing Ras Tafari, later to become Haile Selassie, walk up the Legation steps when he brought his infant son to my father for safe-keeping, before he went north to give final battle; hearing the mass rifle-fire in the town, celebrating the news of overwhelming victory.

Two days later the army came in. Throughout the day they poured past the Royal Pavilion to the thunder of war drums and the blare of trumpets. They were still frenzied with the excitement of that desperate battle, when sixty thousand men fought hand to hand on the plains around Sagale. The blood on the clothes they had stripped from the dead was barely dry. All of them carried shields and brandished rifles, spears or naked swords. Most of them were in white, but the chiefs were in full panoply of war, lion-mane head-dresses, velvet cloaks of many colours, long silken shirts; their shields were embossed with silver or gilt as were the scabbards of their swords. Above this endless tide of men the banners dipped and danced, red, gold and green, the colours of the Empire. Wave after wave,

In the saddle
with my father, 1914:
during a journey from
Addis Ababa to the distant
railhead, *en route* to the
coast at Jibuti, on home leave.
The railway did not extend
to Addis Ababa till 1917.

1916, year of the successful
rebellion in Abyssinia
against the young uncrowned
Emperor Lij Yasu.
Here are Shoan warriors of
Ras Tafari (later Haile Selassie)
after the battle at Sagale,
when the army of Lij Yasu,
by now deposed, was
finally shattered.

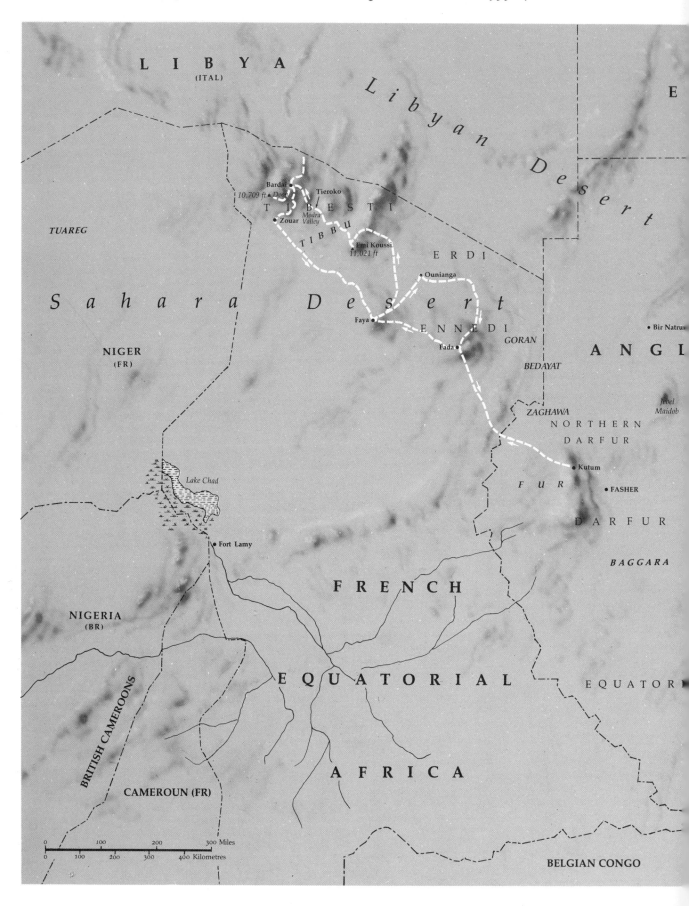

LIBYA
(ITAL)

Libyan Desert

E

TUAREG

Bardai
10,709 ft *Doro
Tieroko
T I B E S T I
Zouar
Modra Valley
T I B B U
Emi Koussi
11,021 ft

ERDI

Ounianga

Sahara   Desert

Faya
E N N E D I
GORAN
Fada
BEDAYAT

A N G L

• Bir Natrun

Jebel Maidob

ZAGHAWA
NORTHERN
DARFUR

NIGER
(FR)

Kutum
F U R
• FASHER

D A R F U R

BAGGARA

Lake Chad

• Fort Lamy

F R E N C H

NIGERIA
(BR)

E Q U A T O R I A L

EQUATOR

A F R I C A

BRITISH CAMEROONS

CAMEROUN (FR)

0   100   200   300 Miles
0   100   200   300   400 Kilometres

BELGIAN CONGO

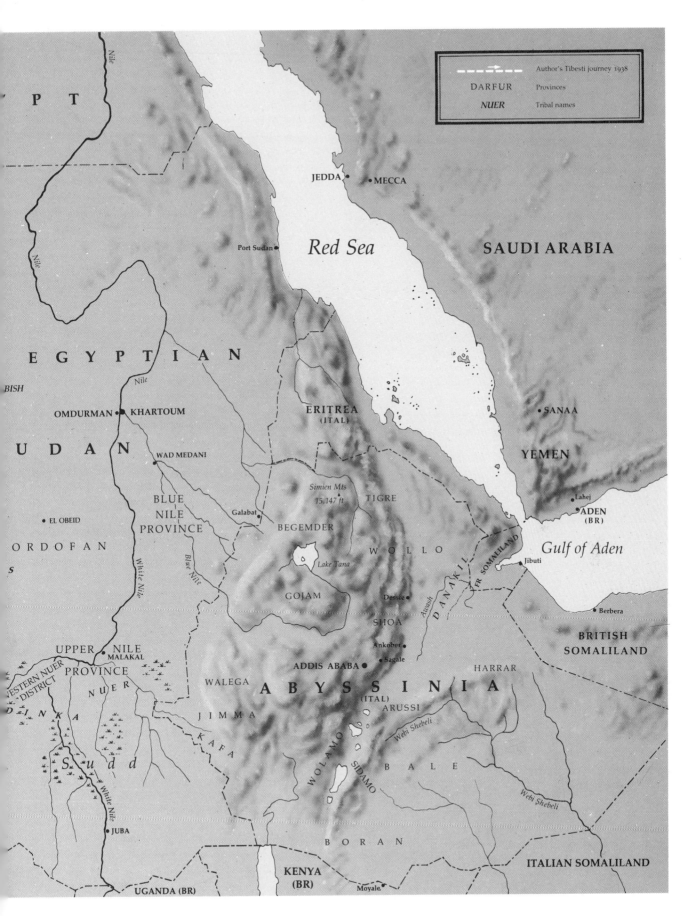

Soldiers of the conquering Shoan army, celebrating the triumph they had won at the homeric battle of Sagale, 27th October 1916.

In the Addis Ababa marketplace, 1916. Public hangings were not uncommon, and attracted little attention from passers-by.

horsemen and men on foot, mixed in seeming confusion, they surged past throughout the day, thrusting close to the steps of the Pavilion to boast of their prowess, while the Court Chamberlains beat them back with wands. Negus Michael was led past with a stone on his shoulder in token of submission, an old man in a black *burnous* with a white cloth wrapped about his head. Ras Lul Seged's young son came past at the head of a few hundred men, all that were left of the five thousand who had fought beside his father at Ankober. I remember the excited face of a boy, seemingly little older than myself, who was carried past in triumph. He had killed two men. At last it was over – a small English boy had watched a sight as barbaric and enthralling as was ever seen in Africa.

My father was due for leave, but in 1917 it was impossible for him to take his family back to England, so we went to India instead, where his brother, Lord Chelmsford, was Viceroy. On the way we visited Berbera in British Somaliland, where fighting was going on against the Dervish forces under the Mad Mullah. From there we went to Aden in a gunboat and I was desperately seasick. We stayed with General Stewart in the Residency, and he took us up to the trenches at Lahej. I remember Sikh troops in grey shirts and turbans, and how I stood on a pile of sandbags to watch shells bursting over the Turkish lines. Then on to Delhi, an odd mixture of memories – servants in splendid uniforms, squirrels scampering about, the grey pony which threw me off at a gymkhana, the Red Fort, men bathing in the Jumna river, dense crowds in strange-looking clothes, how impressive my uncle looked in his state robes, cavalry at a review, and the music of military bands. We stayed with the Maharajah in Jaipur. There, from an elephant, I watched pig-sticking, went in an ox cart to shoot blackbuck, watched wild animals fighting in an arena. I can still see a man at the Palace gates with a cheetah on a chain; a sambur stag galloping past during a drive for panther; and the wonderful peacocks. I shall never forget sitting, very still, in a *machan*, hearing the beaters getting closer. Then a nudge and looking down to see the tiger, unexpectedly red, move forward just below us.

18

A group at the British Legation, Addis Ababa, February 1917, on the occasion of the Coronation of the Empress Zauditou, who came to the throne after Lij Yasu's deposition. I am the child on the ground in front. My father and mother are seated behind. Between them are my brothers (*left to right*) Brian, Dermot and Roderic. Among others in the group are (*directly behind my mother*) Mr (later Sir Gerald) Campbell, Consul at Addis Ababa, and Mrs Campbell; and (*extreme right*) Mr (later Sir Arnold) Hodson, Consul for Southern Abyssinia; and (*tall figure on my mother's left*) Mr (later Sir Geoffrey) Archer, Commissioner, British Somaliland.

England and Abyssinia 1919–33

We returned to England from Addis Ababa early in 1919 and I saw British troops on the banks of the Suez Canal. Then one brother and I were sent to a boarding school on the Sussex coast, between the cold, grey sea and the bleached, bleak downs. Till then I had hardly met any English children other than my brothers. I think I was a friendly, responsive child but utterly ignorant of the rigid conventions that govern schoolboy society. On my first day I went round calling out, 'Has anyone seen Brian?', instead of 'Thesiger minor'; and I was not allowed to forget this appalling solecism. As far as the other boys were concerned we were freaks. We had never kicked a ball about, barely heard of a game called cricket. I spoke of things that I had seen and done and was promptly called a liar. 'Have you heard what Thesiger major says? He says he was in the trenches in the War.' Inevitably I was driven in upon myself, acquired a deep-seated mistrust of my contemporaries, and became quarrelsome and aggressive. I can remember fighting with a boy called Lucas: I had him by the throat and by the time I was dragged off him he was unconscious. This did not increase my popularity. My father died during my second term, which added to my desolation. The headmaster was a sadist. He had certain victims, my brother and myself among them, and on the slightest excuse, such as making a noise in the passage or not putting our shoes away properly, he beat us with a whip with a red lash. I carried the marks for years. These early beatings certainly hardened me, so that later at Eton, where I was beaten repeatedly and deservedly, I regarded the conventional 'tannings' and even the occasional birchings almost as a joke. Eton, for which I acquired a deep and lasting affection, gave me the privacy of a room to myself in civilised surroundings, but I was still at odds with my contemporaries, which was a pity, depriving me of much that Eton had to offer. I went on to Magdalen College, Oxford, where I was more successful. There I discovered that people are prepared to be friendly if you give them a chance; but it had been a long hard road. Yet Oxford has never meant as much to me as Eton.

Aged seventeen, at Eton, 1927/28.

During my first long vacation from Oxford I worked my passage as a stoker on a tramp steamer to Constantinople and to Constanza in the Black Sea. In Athens I spent two days on the Acropolis, where the only other person was a shepherd boy with his goats. I came back overland to my home on the Welsh border, which had always been a haven, and there I found a personal invitation from Haile Selassie, requesting me, as my father's eldest son, to attend his Coronation, with a notification from the Foreign Office that I was to be attached to the Duke of Gloucester's Official Mission. This invitation, which so easily might not have been extended, and a later one, even more fortuitous, to go to Arabia, were decisive events in my life. Certainly it is inconceivable that I should have settled to a conventional life in England. At school I had been able to withdraw into a world of my own, rimmed by the mountains of my childhood, Erer, Fantali, Zuqala, Wochercher, Entoto. For me there is still magic in their names. I had read every book I could find on African hunting and travel, by Selous, Gordon-Cumming, Baldwin and others.

A 1930 Legation group for Haile Selassie's Coronation. (*Left to right*) *1st row* Sir Harold Kittermaster (Governor, Somaliland); Sir Sidney Barton (Minister, Addis Ababa); HRH Duke of Gloucester; Sir John Maffey (Governor-General, Sudan); Admiral Fullerton (East Indies Station RN) *2nd row 1–4* Sir Stewart Symes (Resident, Aden); Lord Airlie; H. A. (later Sir Harold) MacMichael (Civil Secretary, Sudan); J. M. (later Sir John) Troutbeck (1st Secretary) *3rd row 2 & 3* Majors R. E. Cheeseman (Consul) & A. T. Miles (ADC) *4th row 1 & 3* P. Zaphiro (Oriental Secretary); myself *5th row 1* E. A. (later Sir Edwin Chapman-Andrews (Vice-Consul).

A contrasting style of dignity, 1917: a group of the Abyssinian nobility in their full dress, the style of which remained unchanged in 1930.

But without this invitation my inevitable quest for adventure would have taken a different path. Now I was on my way back to Abyssinia, with a rifle in my baggage.

We landed at Jibuti from HMS *Effingham*, after a formal dinner in the Admiral's cabin, and caught the train to Addis Ababa. Along the length of the train and thrown into sharp relief by the flickering oil lamps, jostled a bedlam of porters in loincloths, with long hair or shaven skulls, arguing in guttural Somali. Behind them were the onlookers, slender figures in white robes and rich turbans, silent and impassive against the night. As I climbed into my compartment I felt drunk with excitement.

In Addis Ababa the compound and the Legation building seemed smaller; only the trees were larger, shutting out the mountains. The kites still shrilled above the eucalyptus trees and the same blue, pungent smoke rose over the servants' quarters. It needed a conscious effort to remember Eton, Oxford and my home in Radnorshire. I could not believe that I had been away for more than ten years. Only the servants, when they came forward to welcome me, led by Hapta Woldt, my personal *syce* who had held me on my pony at the age of three, were grey and grizzled by the passage of the years.

I stayed in one of a row of tents pitched in the Legation paddock. Fourteen years before I had stood there and watched the armies passing north to war. Now they were passing once again, but this time from the north. Many of them had been marching for weeks over the bare, high plateau and the tremendous gorges that cut across it. Each contingent followed its immediate chief, and he in turn followed his Dejazmatch or Ras from Tigre, Wollo or Begemder. The great feudal lords rode magnificently caparisoned mules, their draped war-horses following behind, and they moved in a crush of retainers, part of the flood of armed men pouring into the town. We were woken at dawn by their trumpets. Other armies were entering, from Gojam and Walega in the west, from Harrar, from Arussi and Bale, and from provinces of the captive south, coming in to Addis Ababa to pay allegiance to Haile Selassie at his crowning as King of Kings.

For ten hectic days we took part in processions, ceremonies and banquets, and finally watched the Patriarch crown and anoint Haile Selassie with the ritual of his Church, one of the oldest in Christendom. Then, under the state umbrella, with his crown upon his head, he came out into the square to show himself to his people, the latest in that long line of kings that claimed descent from Solomon and Sheba. From every corner of the Empire they were there to pay him homage. They stood before him, magnificent in brilliant robes and lion-mane head-dresses, their shields gleaming with gold and silver. They wore great curved swords, with which many had fought for him at Sagale. Perhaps I was conscious even then that traditions, customs and rites, long cherished and revered, would soon be discarded, that the colour and variety that distinguished this scene would disappear from the land for ever. Already there were a few cars in the streets. There had been none when I was a boy.

The last ceremonies were over and the crowds were going home. I still had two months before I was due back at Oxford. Helped by Colonel Sandford, an old family friend who had lived in Addis Ababa for years, I collected servants to take me down into the Danakil country. This was unadministered and dangerous territory, for the Danakil had a fearsome reputation. I planned to follow the

Emperor Haile Selassie
wearing his State Crown
after his Coronation,
November 1930.

21

Awash river northward to the hot springs of Bilen, and then to return eastward across the desert. As the telegraph poles along the railway dropped out of sight I knew I was now on my own, that if things went wrong I could get no help. I would not have had it otherwise, as I followed the camels loaded with my tent and stores through the acacia scrub, at this season bare except for thorns. We camped in the shade of great fig trees on the river bank; crocodiles sunned themselves nearby on the sandbanks, and hippopotamus grunted in the deeper pools. The Danakil, after watering their camels, collected round our camp. Slender figures in short loincloths, their mops of hair dressed with melted butter, they had open, attractive faces, but each of them wore across his stomach a large, curved dagger from which hung leather thongs, one for each man that he had killed and castrated.

I had everything I wanted, even more than I had dreamed of as a boy poring over *Jock of the Bushveld*. Here were herds of oryx and Soemerings gazelle on the plains, waterbuck in the tamarisk along the river, lesser kudu and gerenuk in the thick bush, and greater kudu, trophy of trophies, among the isolated mountains. Here were the camp fires and the noises of the night, the voices of my Somalis, the brilliant African stars, the moonlight on the river, the chill wind of dawn, the hot still noons, mirages transforming the parched plains into phantom lakes, dust-devils spiralling through the bush, vultures circling over the camp, guinea-fowl calling among the trees, and the loading and unloading of camels. Back at Oxford I would remember the satisfaction of a successful stalk, a clean kill and a good head, the dry mouth and weariness after a long hunt, the last dragging miles into camp, the weight of the rifle on my shoulder, the sight of the camp fires, the satisfaction of a cup of hot tea, a bath, then grilled steaks for dinner. I was to remember a sudden blinding rainstorm that filled a dry watercourse in a few seconds with a raging torrent of water, and almost overnight the magic transformation of seemingly lifeless bush into green parkland; and to remember clearly the mixed feelings of fear and excitement when a band of Itu Galla surrounded our camp and shouted defiance, while some baboons scampered up an adjacent cliff face. Then the telegraph poles rose again across the plain and we were back on the railway line. I paid off my caravan and rode up to Harrar, hardly changed since Burton's visit of 1855. I returned to Europe from Jibuti, third class in a *Messageries Maritimes* boat packed with soldiers of the Foreign Legion.

Back in Oxford I spent hours thinking about the Awash river, which never reached the sea. Its disappearance, somewhere in Danakil country, posed the last important problem of African discovery, trifling in comparison with the search for the sources of the Nile, but still challenging in an age of vanishing opportunity. Late in the last century three expeditions, led by Munzinger, Giulietti and Bianchi, had been wiped out by the Danakil. Nesbitt, in 1928, had carried out his great journey through this country, but several of his men had been murdered and he was forced to escape westward from Bahdu. He had later travelled northward across the lava deserts and had left the problem of the river's disappearance unsolved. I made up my mind to follow the Awash to its end. But sometimes at night, especially after I had been reading Nesbitt's account in the *Geographical Journal*, I felt distinctly apprehensive.

I took my History finals in 1933, though I fear my reading for the examination took second place to preparations for my journey. I then returned to Abyssinia, accompanied by David Haig-Thomas.

An Oxford photograph: I boxed for the University from 1930 to 1933 (and was captain in my last year).

We travelled first to the Arussi mountains. Visible and alluring from the Legation, these mountains were a week's journey away. Now they are only an hour or two by car and the forests are gone. For three months we travelled there, hunting mountain nyala, a most elusive quarry in the giant heath above the forests or higher still among the giant lobelias where clouds formed and reformed, allowing only glimpses of the Rift Valley seven thousand feet below. We travelled through forests where black and white colobus monkeys swung through the lichen-covered trees, and we rode across wide plains near the headwaters of the Webi Shebeli. Then we dropped off the Chercher mountains to the desert's edge.

David Haig-Thomas was suffering from acute laryngitis and when we reached the railway he decided to go back to England. I was glad to see him go, for though we never quarrelled I found his presence an irritant and was happy now to be on my own. This was no fault of his, for he was good-natured and accommodating. Like many English travellers I find it difficult to live for long periods with my own kind. On later journeys I was to find comradeship among Arabs and Africans, the very differences between us binding me more closely to them. No-one has ever mattered to me more than some of the friends I made among them, as I discovered to my cost years later when one of them died. On this journey, however, I still had a sense of racial superiority, acquired in my childhood, which set me apart from the men who followed me. Even Omar, my Somali headman, on whom I was utterly dependent, was in no sense a companion.

I started from the Awash station with eighteen camels and some forty armed men, *Danakil country 1933–34* including an escort of twelve provided by the Government. Most of my men were Somalis from several different tribes, but I also had with me Amhara, Galla and Gurages, some of whom were Christians. The rest were Muslims. I heard a rumour that the Government, as a result of recent fighting among the Danakil, was going to forbid my departure. We therefore left as quickly as possible. I realised that we could not hope to force our way through the Danakil country. Other, far better armed, expeditions had come to grief there, but I hoped we should be too strong to invite attack and yet not so strong as to provoke it.

Among the Danakil a man's standing in his tribe depended to a very large extent on the number of men or boys, however young, that he had killed and castrated. Decorations, such as an ostrich feather or a wooden comb in the hair, a necklace, an iron bracelet, or an ivory armband, as well as the number of thongs hanging from the scabbard of his dagger, showed at a glance how often a man had killed. To kill was what counted; how, was of little importance. This seemed to me fair enough; it would never have occurred to me deliberately to attract the attention of a lion before I fired at it.

The Galla tribes, even in Kenya, castrate their victims, but what made the Danakil so dangerous was that so many of them, even boys, carried rifles, which had been smuggled into the country through French Somaliland. The Danakil were divided into the Asaimara, the Red Men, who were the nobility, and the Adoimara, or White Men. The Asaimara inhabited Bahdu and Aussa and were the more formidable. Nesbitt barely escaped from Bahdu, and as we approached Mount Ayelu, which dominates it, we were repeatedly warned by the Adoimara that we should most certainly be killed if we went there. A number of ruined encampments along our route, wiped out by the Asaimara, lent force to their arguments.

The Danakil Country 1930–34

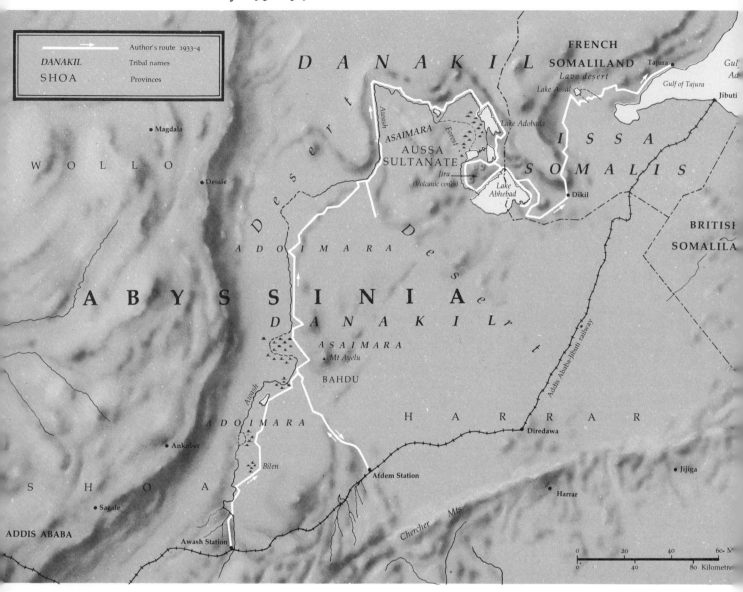

Legend:

DANAKIL — Tribal names
SHOA — Provinces
——→ Author's route 1933–4

FRENCH SOMALILAND
DANAKIL
Lava desert
Tajura
Gulf of Tajura
Lake Assal
Gul
Aa
Jibuti
ISSA SOMALIS
Magdala
ASAIMARA
Ataush
Forest
Lake Adobada
AUSSA SULTANATE
WOLLO
Dessie
Jira
(Volcanic cones)
Lake Abhebad
Dikil
Desert
ADO IMARA
Desert
BRITISH SOMALILA
ABYSSINIA
DANAKIL
Desert
ASAIMARA
Mt Ayelu
BAHDU
Ataush
ADOIMARA
Addis Ababa–Jibuti railway
HARRAR
Diredawa
Ankober
Bilen
Afdem Station
Jijiga
Harrar
SHOA
Sagale
Chercher Mts
ADDIS ABABA
Awash Station

0   20   40   60 M
0   40   80 Kilometre

24

The fertile plain of Bahdu is entered from the south by a narrow pass between a rocky escarpment and a marsh. We picketed this at dawn and were through before the Asaimara were aware of our approach. We hurriedly pitched camp by the river and built a breastwork. Our arrival caused great excitement and our camp was soon surrounded by a large and ever-growing crowd of warriors. As yet they evinced no sign of hostility, but various remarks, overheard by one of my men who spoke their language, were not reassuring. We spent a tense watchful night but nothing happened. Next day I met the most influential of their chiefs, a nearly blind and very old man who, at last, agreed to give us a safe conduct through Bahdu and a guide to the Sultanate of Aussa, where the river was reported to end. Well pleased, I was sitting in my tent when I was disturbed by shouting outside. A letter had arrived from the Government, passed on from chief to chief. It was addressed to me, but had been handed to the head of my escort and, since he had read it aloud, it was impossible to conceal its contents. I was ordered to return at once and in no circumstances to try to enter Bahdu; if I refused my escort were to return without me. They, of course, were delighted. They had not come with me from choice. I was infuriated by this unwarranted interference that had wrecked my journey, just as all was going well. I realised that even if I could persuade some of my men to come with me it would be suicide to go on. All I could do was to go back to Addis Ababa and try to get this order rescinded. To save time we cut across the desert to the nearest station on the railway line, passing another large encampment which the Asaimara had wiped out only a short while before.

I spent six frustrating weeks in Addis Ababa before I received permission to start again. The authorities insisted that I should give them a letter absolving them from responsibility if I were killed. Obviously this letter would not affect me, but the British Minister was reluctant to agree, feeling that it might later be used as a precedent. In return for the letter I asked for and obtained the release of Miram Muhammad, the head chief of Bahdu, who had been imprisoned when he visited Asba Tafari. Accompanied by him I was welcomed back in Bahdu. There I met an engaging young man called Hamdo Uga. Although he had by then only killed once he had succeeded his father as chief, despite the opposition of some of his people. When I arrived at his village he had recently returned with three more gory trophies. Hamdo Uga wore the decorations to which he was now entitled with conscious pride, like a young officer who had been awarded the MC. We stayed near his village and profited from the feasting. Two days after we left, his village was surprised and I heard that he had been killed. I was sorry, for he had a shy friendliness and undeniable charm.

Six weeks later we camped on the edge of dense forest on the borders of Aussa. It was here that Nesbitt had met Muhammad Yayu, the Sultan, and had been given permission to continue his journey across the desert to the north. My object, however, was to follow the river through Aussa in order to discover where it ended. The Sultan, not unnaturally, feared and mistrusted all Europeans. The French and Italians had occupied great areas along the coast, barren wastes of lava and salt flats; now he suspected that they had designs on the fertile plains of Aussa. Somewhere ahead of me Munzinger and others had died attempting to penetrate this forbidden land.

We remained isolated in our camp. On the third day we heard the sound of distant trumpets and a little later, as the sun set, we were informed that the Sultan

In Bahdu, Danakil country,
1934: two Asaimara tribesmen.
On the left is the
young chieftain, Hamdo Uga,
killed in an inter-tribal
raid a few days later.
To the initiated eye,
the sartorial trimmings of
these men would at once reveal
how many people they
had each killed.

LEFT] December 1933:
the start of my expedition
through Danakil country to
the French Somali coast.
I set out from Awash Station
with forty Somalis and
Abyssinians, and eighteen
camels of which only four
survived the journey.

was waiting to receive me. Accompanied by Omar and some of my men I followed our guide along a narrow track through the darkening forest. Then, unexpectedly, we came to a large clearing, lit by the full moon, where four hundred men in clean white loincloths and all armed with rifles and daggers were formed up behind the Sultan. A small but commanding figure, he was dressed in a long white gown with a shawl over his shoulders and a silver-hilted dagger at his waist. He rose from a low stool and stood awaiting my approach. I greeted him in carefully rehearsed Arabic. He replied and motioned to me to be seated on another stool. His expression was proud and imperious but not cruel, and he had great dignity. He asked some questions but spoke little and never smiled. There were long periods of silence. I was very conscious that all my hopes, even our lives, depended upon the whim of this man. I wondered anxiously about the outcome, but at the same time was thrilled by this dramatic meeting in the moonlit forests of unexplored Africa.

We met again the following morning in the same place. I presented him with two sacks of coffee beans, unprocurable here, and later he sent five oxen to my camp. After more discussion and a number of searching questions, he granted me permission to follow the river through Aussa. Why he gave me this permission, never previously accorded to a European, I do not know.

We marched along the shore of Adobada; alive with crocodiles, the lake lapped the sheer cliffs of Gumare; we passed through forests, round swamps and other lakes, and skirted the volcanic cones of Jira. Then we passed out of Aussa and back once more into the desert. Ahead of us was a great sheet of bitter water, set in a landscape of black rock, and it was here the river ended. Some Danakil took me to a low promontory and showed me where their fathers had wiped out an army of 'Turks' and thrown their guns into the lake. So this was where Munzinger and his men had died, in this dead world of calcined rock and caustic water.

I crossed the border into French Somaliland and stayed with Capitaine Bernard in the fort which he commanded at Dikil. He and most of his men were to die a few months later, ambushed by a force from Aussa. From Dikil I set out to cross the lava deserts and salt plains to Tajura on the coast. So far it had been the tribes that menaced us; now it was the land itself. We were lucky, for some recent rain had fallen, but even so of my eighteen camels fourteen were dead before we reached the sea.

This photograph of me was taken by Omar, the Somali headman of my Danakil expedition, three days before we reached the coast, in May 1934.

Sudan Political Service 1935–39

I returned to England, joined the Sudan Political Service and reached Khartoum early in 1935. Having spent nearly half my life in Africa, I was at home among the noises and smells of the market in Addis Ababa, and in the chaos of its crowded streets, where hyaenas scavenged by night. But I felt cheated here in Khartoum, where policemen directed traffic down clean straight streets, where officials kept office hours, hostesses gave formal dinner parties, and newcomers dropped cards in boxes labelled *In* and *Out*. Fortunately I was sent to Kutum in Northern Darfur, where I was privileged to serve under Guy Moore. Before I left Khartoum well-meaning people had warned me that he was very odd, had no regard for time, whether for meals or in his office, and lived and travelled hard. I welcomed the prospect.

Northern Darfur, of some fifty thousand square miles, was the largest District in the Sudan. To the north it merged with the Libyan desert; to the west it bordered on the French Sahara. It was inhabited by a variety of tribes, Arab,

Berber and negro, some of whom were nomadic, all of whom were interesting. Among them I made many friends.

Guy Moore was the only other Englishman in the District, and six months after I had arrived he went on leave and left me in charge. We were always thankful that we had no wireless communication with Provincial Headquarters at Fasher. The mail arrived by runner once a week. We had a lorry and a small truck but travelled nearly always by camel and spent most of our time touring the District.

Moore, a tubby, talkative man with a red face and very blue eyes, fully lived up to his reputation. Always up at sunrise, he might not go to the office till ten but frequently stayed there till five or six without a break. He would dine any time between ten and midnight. We were seldom both in Kutum but when we were we dined together, in his house or mine, and then we would sit talking into the early hours. He was a man of great humanity and understanding, devoted to the people whom he served. He was sure the harm that comes from sudden change far outweighs the good. After the First World War he had served in the deserts of Iraq where his experience of nomad Arabs gave him a different outlook from most District Commissioners in the Sudan. I was fascinated by his stories of the Arabian desert.

He taught me to travel light and to regard not as servants but as companions the men who accompanied me. Soon after I arrived he took me with him 'on trek'. We rode long hours and fed only at sunset. I had never ridden a camel until I came to Kutum but I felt that I was being challenged and I responded. More conventional DCs took with them tents, beds, chairs, tables and cook-boxes loaded on a string of camels, and a retinue of servants. I learnt to sleep on the ground under the stars and to feed with my right hand from a common dish with my companions. Accepted practice in Arabia, such behaviour was unheard of in the Sudan Service, whose pattern came from India.

I soon exchanged for riding camels the baggage camels that I had taken over from my predecessor, acquiring the best that I could get, one in particular was famous. On this camel I once rode a hundred and fifteen miles in twenty-three hours; and from Jebel Maidob to Omdurman in nine days, four hundred and fifty miles in a straight line but nearer six hundred as we went. For a month I travelled in the Libyan desert, going as far as Bir Natrun, the only wells in that region. This was a new world. Hour after hour, day after day we moved forward and nothing changed. Always the same distance ahead desert met empty sky. Round us was silence where only the winds played, and cleanness infinitely remote from the world of men.

I spent all my spare time hunting. I shot oryx and addax in the Libyan desert, stalked Barbary sheep on the crater hills of Maidob and hunted lion wherever I could find them. Lion were accounted vermin in the Sudan in those days; in Northern Darfur they very largely fed off the tribesmen's herds. With Idris, a Zaghawa lad who was my personal retainer and a brilliant tracker, I followed their spoor for hours across stony hills and gravel plains. Idris and I rode down lion on horses with the Bani Hussain. This tribe belonged to the great Baggara confederacy of pastoral, cattle-owning Arabs who had been the mainstay of the Khalifa's army, and had fought with dauntless courage at Omdurman, seeking to match their swords and spears against Kitchener's artillery and machine guns.

They brandished their great shovel-headed spears and shouted defiance at the cornered lion as they circled the cover where they had driven it to bay. Left to

Northern Darfur District, Anglo-Egyptian Sudan, 1936: tribesmen, posed with two of the many lions I shot there, at a time when lion, largely preying on the tribal herds, were numerous enough to be accounted vermin.

Western Nuer District, Upper Nile Province, 1938–39: the stern-wheel steamer *Kerreri* which, with a barge lashed to its side, served as the mobile headquarters of this district on the Nile, in which waterways and marsh predominated.

themselves they would have dismounted and met its charge on their spears. They had no shields and one or more would have been killed, and others mauled. I lacked the nerve to join them in this. Instead, as soon as I could discern the lion's shape among the bushes, I jumped off my horse, let it go and shot the lion, generally as it charged from close quarters. I shot thirty lions during my two years in Northern Darfur.

Before going on leave in 1937 I heard I was to be transferred to Wad Medani, the cotton-growing area on the Blue Nile. I was appalled at the prospect. Fortunately I was able to persuade Angus Gillan, the Civil Secretary, to let me resign from the permanent Political Service and rejoin on a contract, with the understanding that I should only serve in the wilds. Returning from leave, part of which was spent in Morocco, I found I had been posted to the Western Nuer District of the Upper Nile. This District was in the heart of the Sudd, the great swampland of Equatoria. Only since 1925 had the area been administered. The first District Commissioner had been killed and there had been fierce fighting before the Nuer finally submitted. Now there were not even regular police in the District, only tribal police who carried spears instead of rifles, were naked like their kinsmen, but distinguished from them by a badge on their arms.

My District Commissioner was Wedderburn-Maxwell, a jovial, imperturbable man, happily content to live among his naked subjects in a domain of reeds and water. Our headquarters was the *Kerreri*, a paddle-steamer with a barge tied alongside. On this we would steam up and down the main channel of the Nile and its branches, bordered by impenetrable swamp, the papyrus nearly as tall as the *Kerreri*. Here were crocodiles and hippopotamus, the rare situtunga antelope, ungainly shoe-billed storks and, when the river was low, concentrations of elephant. We would tie up at one of the few landing places, go ashore with our porters, and travel for weeks across endless grass plains alive with herds of antelope and dotted with cattle camps. There were no other buildings, no roads, hardly a discernible track. Then we would meet the *Kerreri* again somewhere else. The Governor in Malakal only required a letter about once a month, to let him know we were all right. We kept a few files for our own convenience but were not

On trek in Nuer country, 1938:
I have shot an elephant,
and my porters are
cutting up the meat.

A tribesman of
Western Nuer District,
in papyrus swamp
typical of
the region.
These fine people were
a naked tribe.

bothered by the paperwork of more conventional Districts. The District was lightly administered and our main preoccupation was to deter the warlike Nuer from the constant temptation of raiding their Dinka neighbours.

Strikingly beautiful people, the Nuer were completely naked except for the married women who wore a fringe round their waists. The men, who were exceptionally tall, with slender, well-proportioned bodies and fine features, wore their hair long and often dyed it a golden colour with cow's urine. They owned great herds of cattle, round which their lives centred and with which they identified themselves completely, each man being called after his 'name ox'. Intensely proud, they did not lie or steal, and had the strict code of morality that is so often found with nakedness and tends to disappear with it. Friendly and forthcoming, they cast a spell over the Englishmen who served among them.

I shot meat for the porters and hunted lion, elephant and buffalo for sport. The Nuer greatly prized the meat and fat of the hippopotamus, which they harpooned from small, floating islands of soggy vegetation. On one occasion I went with them and acquired some prestige by spearing and killing a hippopotamus myself as it charged us through the water at the end of thirty feet of rope. Once was enough for me. This incessant killing sounds reprehensible today, but it can only be judged in the context of the past, when this part of Africa was alive with animals, and it was possible to see a thousand elephant in one day. The few score animals that I shot, largely for meat, were fewer than the toll taken by a pride or two of lions during the same time. Recently in Kenya I have done what I could, as an Honorary Game Warden, towards the conservation of wildlife, but it would be hypocrisy to pretend that I regret those distant golden days. I had no white hunter at my side when I followed a wounded lion into long grass or faced an angry elephant. Time and again I stumbled back to camp bone-weary, and often unsuccessful. Such hunting bore no resemblance to the safaris that I encountered years later in East Africa, equipped with cars, lorries, radios and refrigerators and organised by professional hunters.

In Darfur I had heard the Zaghawa speak of the great mountains of Tibesti far away in the west where the Tibbu lived. Nachtigal had failed to get there in 1869, and only French officers on duty had been there since. These officers and their escort

A Tibbu guide, Tibesti.

The Sahara, 1938:
one of the gorges in the
great Tibesti mountains,
Northern Chad,
which I reached
with a camel expedition
from Darfur in the Sudan.

Khartoum, December 1940:
I am talking to the exiled
Emperor Haile Selassie, at the
beginning of the campaign
to liberate Abyssinia and
restore him to his throne.

War 1939–45

of *Goums* still crossed the desert on camels from Fort Lamy to Tibesti, Erdi and
Ennedi, and when I went to Tibesti on leave in the summer of 1938 no mechanised
transport had ever penetrated this part of the Sahara. Two or three years later the
Long Range Desert Group drove all over this desert in jeeps and lorries, to be
followed by Leclerc's force going north from Chad.

I was accompanied by Idris and an elderly Bedayi who, having lived among the
Tibbu as a child, knew their language. We did long marches, sometimes riding for
eighteen and twenty hours. At last we saw, like a cloud upon the desert's edge,
the faint outline of Emi Koussi, the crater summit of Tibesti. As we drew near, it
dominated our world, sharp blue at dawn but dark against the setting sun. We
climbed it with difficulty and at last, eleven thousand feet above sea-level, stood
on the crater's rim. We travelled across wind-swept uplands, over passes and
through narrow gorges, under precipices and past towering peaks. We visited the
great crater of Doon, two thousand five hundred feet in depth, and camped in the
Modra valley beneath Tieroko, most magnificent of all the Tibesti mountains. We
stayed among the Tibbu in their palm groves and in their spartan encampments
among the mountains. They had been great raiders in the past, endlessly at war
with the Tuareg to the west. On our way back to the Sudan we passed the three
strange lakes of Ounianga, one red, one blue and one green. When we got back
to Kutum, we had ridden over two thousand miles in three months.

I was on leave in England planning to go to Persia when the Second World War
started, but was immediately called back to the Sudan with all other officials who
were on leave. After some preparatory training in Khartoum with the Cheshire
and the Essex Regiments I joined the Sudan Defence Force with a Governor-
General's commission as a *Bimbashi*.

After the Italians entered the war I fought for some months on the frontier at
Galabat and then joined Sandford's 101 Mission in Gojam, which was organising
the Abyssinian Patriot resistance to the Italians. I later served under Wingate, a
ruthless, uncompromising, Old Testament figure; brutal, arrogant and eccentric,
he provoked needless hostility among his superiors but, inspired with a burning
faith in his mission, he achieved the seemingly impossible during this campaign.
For me the liberation of Abyssinia had the quality of a crusade. Ten years earlier I

had watched Haile Selassie being crowned in Addis Ababa; six years after that, at Victoria Station, I had seen him descend from the train into exile. I am proud to have served with Sandford's Mission that prepared the way for Haile Selassie's restoration, and to have fought in Wingate's Gideon Force that took him back from the Sudan through Gojam to Addis Ababa. Though eventually deposed, humiliated, maligned and murdered after a lifetime of service to his country, he was one of the great men of our age.

From Addis Ababa I was posted to the Middle East with the rank of Major to help Colonel Gerald de Gaury raise a Druze Legion against the Vichy French in Syria. I joined him at the Arab Legion camp at Azraq, where the castle, built on Roman foundations by the Arabs at the time of the Crusades, still looks out over the marshes. A few days later I crossed the Syrian frontier with a large following of Druze horsemen. As we rode across the lava fields towards the distant mountain, my men roared out the songs their fathers had sung twenty years earlier as they rallied to Sultan Pasha al Atrash, when the war-fires blazed on the village roofs, summoning the Druzes to war; he had led his people from victory to victory against the French, till all Syria had risen in revolt and the French had to assemble two hundred thousand men, bombard Damascus and shell the Street called Straight.

Sultan Pasha had been one of my boyhood heroes. Abd al Karim had been the other, a great Moroccan leader who, at the head of his Riff tribesmen, annihilated the Spanish armies and gave desperate battle to the French, threatening Fez itself. As a boy at Eton I had searched the newspapers daily to see how they fared, and I remember even now my distress as each in turn was overwhelmed.

I remained for six months in Jebel Druze, living in houses some of which had been built by the Romans. I liked the Druzes enormously: they were brave and intensely proud, intelligent, hospitable and very friendly.

It was during this time that I met Sultan Pasha al Atrash. Still commanding immense respect, he took no part in this conflict. Magnanimously, the French had allowed him to return to Jebel Druze and now, in the time of their tribulation, he

Agibar, Abyssinia, June 1941: a Patriot soldier who was with me during Wingate's final rounding-up of the Italian forces which he had driven out of Gojam.

Gojam, Abyssinia, 1941: a group of the Abyssinian Patriots, the resistance forces, armed with captured Italian rifles.

Syria, July 1941:
a Druze cavalryman, serving
in the campaign against
the Vichy French.

remained loyal to his undertakings. Erect, with thoughtful, level gaze, he spoke to me quietly of the past. I found him movingly impressive.

Gerald de Gaury had moved his headquarters to Basra eski Sham. There, in the massive castle built round a Roman theatre by the Saracens to command the Hauran plain, I met a number of Howaitat sheikhs. Auda abu Tayi, that legendary warrior who had fought with Lawrence in the Arab Revolt and ridden beside him in triumph into Damascus, was dead, but his son came to offer the help of his tribe against the French.

I spent a further six months travelling among the tribes in Syria, making plans to remain behind if the Germans invaded the country by way of the Caucasus. I met yet another figure from the past: Nuri ibn Shalan entertained me in his great tribal tent. He was very old, but by no means in his dotage, although he had ruled his tribe for thirty years before Lawrence first met him in 1917. Lawrence described him as 'the great Emir of the Ruwalla, who, after the Sherif and ibn Saud and ibn Rashid, was the fourth figure among the precarious princes of the desert'.

In Africa the deserts in which I had travelled had been blanks in time as well as space. They had no known history, the nomads who inhabited them had no known past. Some bushman paintings, a few disputed references in Herodotus and Ptolemy, and tribal legends of the recent past were all that had come down to us. But in Syria the patina of human history was thick along the desert's edge. Damascus and Aleppo had been old before Rome was founded. Among the towns and villages invasion after invasion had heaped ruin upon ruin and each victory had imposed new conquerors upon the last. But the desert had always been inviolate. There I lived among tribes who claimed descent from Ishmael, and listened to old men who spoke of events of a thousand years ago as if they had happened in their own lifetime. I went among them with belief in my own racial superiority, but in their tents I felt an uncouth and inarticulate barbarian, an intruder from a shoddy and materialistic age. From them I learnt how welcoming and hospitable are the Arabs.

From Syria I went to Cairo and then to the Western Desert with the SAS. We travelled in jeeps and, operating far behind the enemy's lines, attacked their communications by night. We carried food, water and fuel with us; we required nothing from our surroundings. I was in the desert but insulated from it by the jeep in which I travelled. Had we stumbled on the legendary oasis of Zarzura, whose discovery had been the dream of every Libyan explorer, I would have felt but little interest.

In the last year of the war I was back in Abyssinia, at the request of the Emperor, stationed at Dessie as Political Adviser. The country required technicians but had little use for Political Advisers. Frustrated and unhappy, I resigned. In Addis Ababa, quite by chance, I met and dined with O. B. Lean, a desert locust specialist. He said he was looking for someone to collect information on locust outbreak centres in the Empty Quarter of Arabia. I said at once I would love to, but unfortunately I was no entomologist. Lean assured me this was not half so important as knowledge of desert travel. Before we had finished dinner I had been offered and had accepted the job.

All my past had been a prelude to the years that lay ahead.

THE DESERT

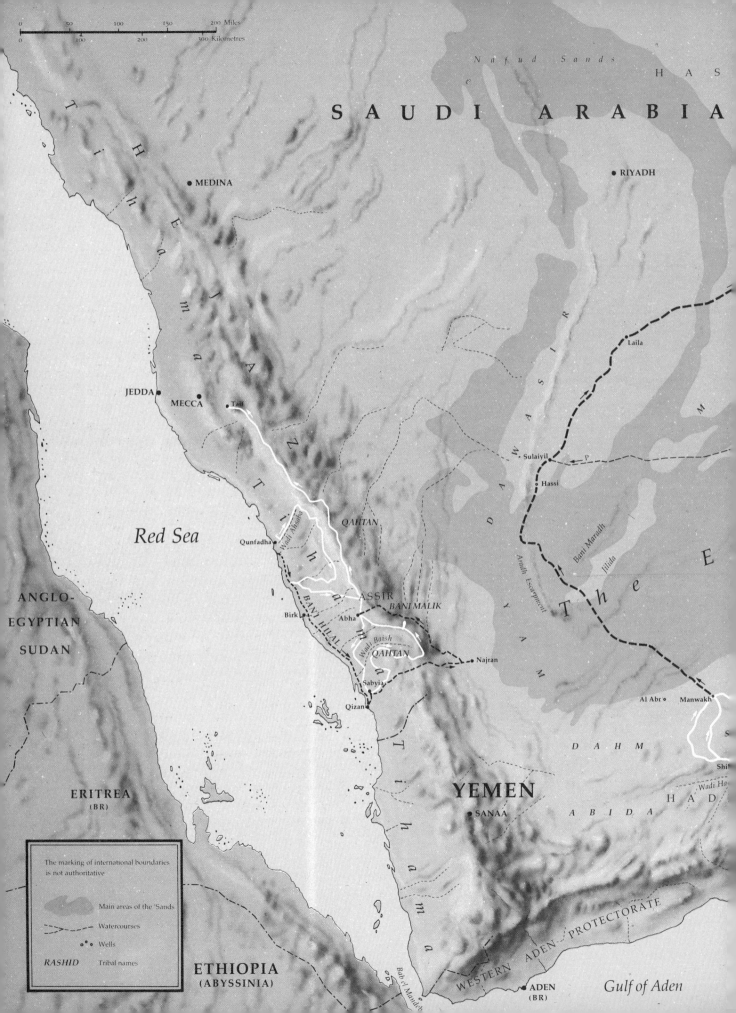

SAUDI ARABIA

• RIYADH

HAS

Nafud Sands

T i h a m a

• MEDINA

JEDDA •
MECCA • • Taif

Red Sea

Qunfadha •

Wadi Ahshán

QAHTAN

ASSIR

BANI MALIK

Birk •

• Abha

Wadi Baish

QAHTAN

Sabyia •

Qizan •

**ANGLO-
EGYPTIAN
SUDAN**

Laila •

D A W A S I R

Sulaiyil •

• Hassi

Aradh Escarpment

Bani Maradh

Jilida

D A H M

T h e

E

Y A M

• Najran

Al Abr • Manwakh •

S

Shi

Wadi Ha

B I D A H A D

YEMEN

T i h a m a

• SANAA

ERITREA
(BR)

Bab el Mandeb

**ETHIOPIA
(ABYSSINIA)**

WESTERN ADEN PROTECTORATE

• ADEN
(BR)

Gulf of Aden

0   50   100   150   200 Miles
0   100   200   300 Kilometres

The marking of international boundaries
is not authoritative

Main areas of the 'Sands

Watercourses

Wells

RASHID   Tribal names

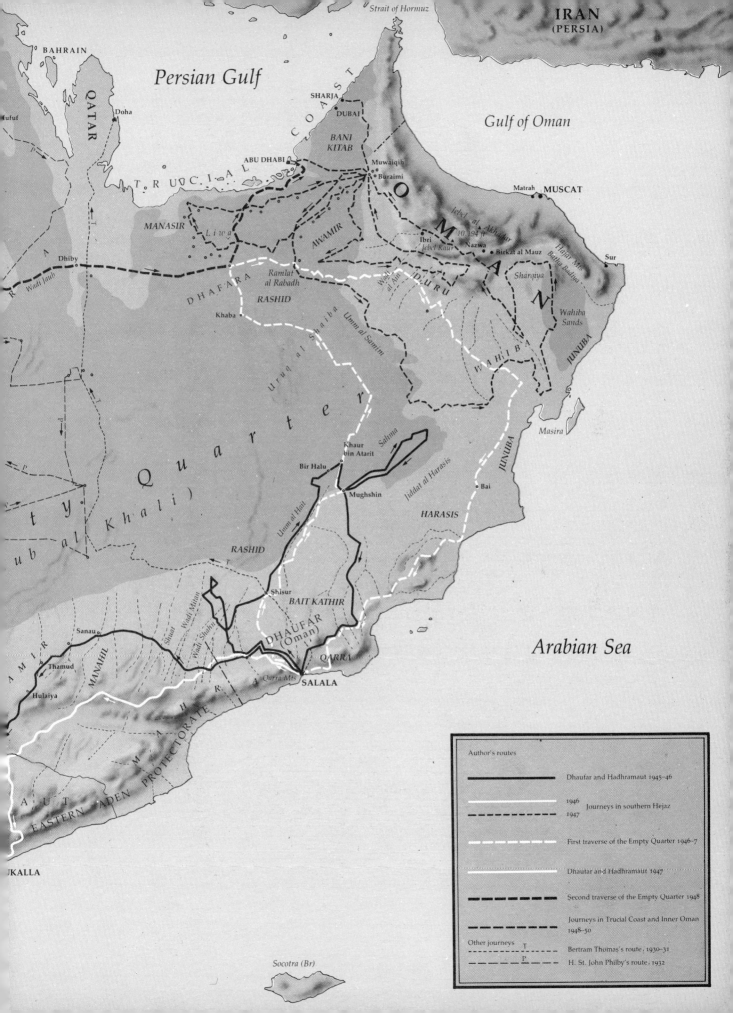

Strait of Hormuz

**IRAN
(PERSIA)**

Persian Gulf

BAHRAIN

QATAR

Doha

SHARJA

DUBAI

BANI
KITAB

ABU DHABI

Muwaiqih

Buraimi

Gulf of Oman

Matrah · **MUSCAT**

T R U C I A L   C O A S T

MANASIR

Liwa

AWAMIR

O

Jebel al Akhdar
10,394 ft

Ibri · *Jebel Kaur*

Nazwa

Birkat al Mauz

M

Hajar Me
Batha Badiya

Sur

Dhiby

Wadi Jauh

DHAFARA

Ramlat
al Rabadh

RASHID

Khaba

DURU

Wadi
al Ain

A

Sharqiya

N

Wahiba
Sands

JUNUBA

R

P

Uruq al Shaiba

Umm al Somim

WAHIBA

d

Masira

Khaur
bin Atarit

Sahma

Bir Halu

Umm al Hait

Mughshin

Jiddat al Harasis

Bai

JUNUBA

t   y

ub al Khali)

Q u a r t e r

RASHID

Arabian Sea

HARASIS

Shisur

BAIT KATHIR

Sanau

Shuat
Wadi Mitan

Wadi Shahn

MANAHIL

Thamud

Hulaiya

DHAUFAR
(Oman)

QARRA

Qarra Mts
SALALA

A M I R

M A H R

E A S T E R N   A D E N   P R O T E C T O R A T E

A U T

KALLA

Socotra (Br)

Author's routes	
━━━━━	Dhaufar and Hadhramaut 1945–46
━━━━━ (white)	1946 Journeys in southern Hejaz
━ ━ ━ ━	1947
┅┅┅┅ (white dash)	First traverse of the Empty Quarter 1946–7
━━━━━ (white)	Dhaufar and Hadhramaut 1947
▬ ▬ ▬ ▬	Second traverse of the Empty Quarter 1948
━ ━ ━ ━	Journeys in Trucial Coast and Inner Oman 1948–50

Other journeys
- - - - - T   Bertram Thomas's route, 1930–31
- - - - - P   H. St. John Philby's route, 1932

The Desert 1945–50

For years the Empty Quarter offered the ultimate challenge of Arabian exploration. Charles Doughty, returning from his dire wanderings in northern Arabia, wrote, 'I never found any Arabian who had aught to tell, even by hearsay, of that dreadful country,' and in 1929 Lawrence suggested to Trenchard that either the R 100 or R 101 should be diverted on a trial flight to India to pass over it. He wrote, 'To go over the Empty Quarter will also be an enormous advertisement for them: it will mark an era in exploration. It will finish our knowledge of the earth. Nothing but an airship can do it, and I want it to be one of ours which gets the plum.'

The Arabian Peninsula is as large as India without the Himalayas, and only some parts of the Yemen and Oman and various scattered areas can be cultivated. The rest is desert, covering nearly a million square miles. The southern part of this desert, a wilderness of sand dunes surrounded by featureless gravel plains even more lifeless, extends for nine hundred miles from the foothills of the Yemen to the mountains of Oman, and for five hundred miles from the Indian Ocean to the Persian Gulf. It is a desert within a desert, which even Arabs call Rub al Khali, or the Empty Quarter.

Bertram Thomas crossed the Empty Quarter from south to north in 1930–31 and next year St John Philby crossed it from the north. But even as late as 1945 no European had been there since Thomas and Philby, no aeroplane had ever flown over it and no car had been nearer to it than the RAF camp at Salala, on the shore of the Indian Ocean, or the townships on the Trucial Coast. In contrast with the Sahara, which the French had long explored, pacified and administered, vast areas of the Empty Quarter were still unexplored and it was surrounded by a no-man's land of warring tribes.

The Bedu tribes in southern Arabia were insignificant in numbers compared with those of central and northern Arabia, where the tents of a single tribe might number thousands. I had seen the Shamar migrating, a whole people on the move, covering the desert with their herds, and I had visited the summer camp of the Ruwalla, a veritable city of black tents. In southern Arabia families moved over great distances seeking pasture for their camels. Only the bushmen of the Kalahari and the aborigines of Australia led a life of comparable hardship.

Dhaufar and the Hadhramaut 1945–46

I arrived in Dhaufar, on the southern coast of Arabia, in October 1945, and stayed in the RAF staging camp near the small town of Salala, where the airmen were strictly confined to their camp to avoid incidents with the tribesmen. I had come to Arabia resolved to explore the Empty Quarter. It was one of the few places left where I could satisfy an urge to go where others had not been. I believed that the circumstances of my life had so trained me that I was qualified to travel there. The Locust Research Centre required me to go to Mughshin on the edge of the Sands and find out if it was a potential outbreak centre for desert locusts. This suited me well. I expected to be away for two or three months. I hoped this journey would give me the opportunity to accustom myself to the country and so win the confidence of the Arabs.

The Wali or Governor insisted that I should be accompanied by thirty of the Bait Kathir tribe, maintaining that where I was going there was danger from raiding parties. I was reluctant to take so many, but was in no position to argue, knowing nothing of local conditions. A fortnight later the Bait Kathir came to fetch me from the RAF camp. Most of them wore only loincloths and were bare-headed, their long hair tangled and unkempt. All were armed with rifles and daggers. My first impression was that they were little better than savages; they looked as primitive as the Danakil.

We camped that night at the foot of the Qarra mountains and sorted ourselves out. Next day we forced our camels along boulder-strewn tracks, among the tangled woods and ravines, until we came at last to the grassy slopes above. Here *cf. p. 65* the Qarra, a strange folk who spoke a language of their own and never ventured far from their mountain fastness, herded small humpless cattle. In the woods were Paradise fly-catchers and brilliant butterflies. I walked to the watershed and found myself standing between two worlds. To the south were green meadows, *cf. p. 62–3* thickets and spreading trees, to the north was empty desert, sand, rocks and a few wisps of withered grass.

During the days to come we lived crowded together in the emptiness of the desert. I was accustomed to some degree of privacy; here I had none. At first I found the Arabic of these Bedu almost incomprehensible, so there were often misunderstandings. Rain had fallen recently and some vegetation had come up. My companions dawdled along, stopping frequently to let their camels graze, and camping after a few hours of this leisurely progress. I suspected that they were deliberately lengthening the journey in order to get more money: they were paid on daily rates. When I protested that we must do proper marches they argued that their camels were in poor condition, which was evident, that they had a long journey ahead of them, and that there was no grazing further on. Next morning *cf. p. 64* we would go for an hour or so, find more grazing and stop once more. Instead of enjoying this easy travel I got increasingly frustrated and irritated. I had yet to learn that Bedu will always sacrifice every consideration to the welfare of their camels. There were many Arabs in the area, attracted by the grazing. A score would collect, sit down without being invited, eat with us and make heavy inroads on our food. Some of them attached themselves to us for days. My Bedu accepted their presence with equanimity, for they would have done exactly the same themselves.

On previous journeys I had commanded respect as an Englishman, and in the Sudan I had the prestige of being a Government official. These Bedu had never heard of the English. All Europeans were known to them collectively as Christians, or more commonly as Infidels. They were prepared to tolerate my presence as a welcome source of revenue, but they never doubted my inferiority. They were Muslims and Bedu. I was neither. Anxious to prove their equal, I wanted no concessions and was irritated when pressed to ride while they still walked, or *cf. p. 61* when they suggested I was thirsty and needed a drink. I wore their clothes – they would never have gone with me otherwise – and went bare-footed as they did. In camp, especially when we had visitors, I sat in the formal way that Arabs sit, and found this unaccustomed position trying. I thought many of their formalities irksome and pointless. Sometimes we shot a gazelle or oryx and then fed well, but our usual fare was unleavened bread, brick hard or soggy, depending how long it had lain in the embers of the fire. On the gravel plains the water from the infrequent wells tasted of camel's urine, but it was even worse when we reached the Sands, where it resembled a strong dose of Epsom salts, fortunately without the same effect.

cf. p. 64

After travelling across country that had suffered twenty-five years of unbroken drought we visited the small uninhabited oasis of Mughshin. Skeletons of trees, brittle powdery branches fallen and half-buried in the sand, and deposits of silt left by ancient floods, marked the course of Umm al Hait, the 'Mother of Life', the great wadi that leads down to Mughshin. Beyond Mughshin we wound our way among dunes that rose above us like mountains. Later we rode, hour after weary hour, across the emptiness that was the Jiddat al Harasis. It was now that I learnt to appreciate my companions and to admire their skills, their uncanny sense of direction and their skill at tracking. One day we passed some wind-blown tracks, to me just a disturbance of the sand. One of our party climbed down from his camel to look, followed them for a while, fingered some droppings and came back. 'Awamir from the north, six of them. They have raided the Junuba on the southern coast and taken three camels. They came by way of Sahma, watered at Mughshin and passed here six days ago.' We had seen no Arabs for seventeen days and were to meet none for another twenty-seven. When we did we heard that six Awamir had raided the Junuba, killed three of them and taken three camels. The only thing we did not already know was that they had killed anyone.

cf. p. 77

After ten weeks journeying we returned to Salala. I enjoyed the days I spent there. It was agreeable to have hot baths and eat well cooked food, to sit at ease in a chair and talk English for a change, but the pleasure was enhanced by the knowledge that I was going back into the desert.

I now planned to travel in company with the Rashid westward to the Hadhramaut, through country that no European had yet penetrated. I had encountered some of the Rashid in the desert and arranged for them to meet me in Salala.

Many tribes lived round the Empty Quarter, or as these Arabs call it 'the Sands'. Among others were the Yam and the Dawasir, who owed allegiance to Abd al Aziz ibn Saud, King of Saudi Arabia; the Saar and the Manahil near the Hadhramaut; the Bait Kathir; the Duru, on the borders of Oman; and the Manasir near the Persian Gulf; but only the Rashid and the Awamir, and in the north the Murra, were at home in the Sands. Some thirty Rashid had been waiting for me when I arrived back at Salala. They were dressed in long Arab shirts and headcloths, dyed a soft russet-brown with the juice of a desert shrub. They wore their clothes with distinction, even when they were in rags. They were small deft men, alert and watchful. Their bodies were lean and hard, tempered in the furnace of the desert and trained to unbelievable endurance. Looking at them I realised that they were very much alive, tense with a nervous energy vigorously controlled. They had been bred from the purest race in the world and lived in conditions where only the hardiest and best could survive. They were as fine-drawn and highly strung as thoroughbreds. Beside them the Bait Kathir lacked the final polish of the inner desert.

It was on this journey that I met Salim bin Kabina. He was to be my inseparable companion during the five years that I travelled in southern Arabia. He turned up when we were watering thirsty camels at a well that yielded only a few gallons an hour. For two days we worked day and night in relays. Conspicuous in a vivid red loincloth he helped us with our task. On the second day he announced that he was coming with me. I told him to find himself a rifle and a camel. He grinned and said that he would find both, and did. He was sixteen years old, about five foot five in height and lightly built. He was very poor, so the hardship of his life had already marked him. His hair was long and always falling into his eyes, especially when he was cooking, and he would sweep it back impatiently with a thin hand. He had very white teeth which showed constantly, for he was always talking and laughing. His father had died years before and it had fallen on bin Kabina to provide for his mother, young brother and infant sister. I had met him at a critical time in his life. Two months earlier he had gone down to the coast for a load of sardines: on the way back his old camel had collapsed and died. 'I wept as I sat there in the dark beside the body of my old grey camel. She was old, long past bearing and very thin, for there had been no rain for a long time, but she was my camel, the only one I had. That night death seemed very close to me and my family.' Then he grinned at me and said, 'God brought you. Now I shall have everything.' Already I was fond of him. Attentive and cheerful, anticipating my wants, he eased the inevitable strain under which I lived. In the still rather impersonal atmosphere of my desert life his comradeship provided the only personal note.

cf. p. 66

We rode slowly westward. There should have been Arabs here, for rain had fallen and there was good grazing in the broad, shallow watercourses that ran down towards the Sands. But the desert was empty, full of fear. Occasionally we saw herdsmen in the distance, hurriedly driving camels across the plain. Some of the Rashid would get off their camels and throw up sand into the air, the accepted sign of peaceful intentions. Then they would ride over and get the news. Always it was of Dahm raiders from the Yemen, who had passed westward a few days before. Some said they were three hundred strong, others a hundred.

cf. p. 66

We were camped on a plain near some acacia bushes among which our scattered camels were grazing. Half a mile to the west were limestone ridges, dark against the setting sun. The Rashid were lined up for the sunset prayer. Suddenly one exclaimed, 'There are men behind that ridge'. They abandoned their prayers. 'The camels! The camels! Get the camels!' Four or five ran off to help the herdsmen, who had already taken alarm. The rest of us took cover behind the scattered loads. A score of mounted men swung out from behind the ridge and raced towards our camels. We opened fire. Bin al Kamam, who lay near me, said, 'Shoot in front of them, I don't know who they are'. I got off five shots. Everyone was firing. Bin Kabina's three rounds were all duds. I could see the exasperation on his face. The raiders sought cover behind a low hill. Our camels were brought in and couched. 'Who are they?' There was general uncertainty. It was agreed that they were not Dahm or Saar, their saddles were different. Some said they were Awamir, perhaps Manahil. No, they were not Mahra, their clothes were wrong. A Manahil who was with us said he would go and find out. He went forward to the low hill, situated against the glowing sky. We saw a man stand up and come towards him. They shouted to each other and then came together and embraced. They were a Manahil pursuit party following the Dahm, and had seen our camels and taken us for yet another party of Dahm raiders. We had bought a goat that

cf. p. 66

morning which we meant to eat for dinner; instead we feasted the Manahil, who were now our guests.

Six weeks after leaving Salala we were in the valley of the Hadhramaut, and rode slowly up it to Tarim. I was interested to see this famous valley and its unspoilt cities with their distinctive architecture. We were lavishly entertained, sitting indoors in cushioned ease; we ate well cooked food and drank water that did not taste of goatskin. But my companions were anxious to return to the desert. They fretted about their camels that would not eat the clover they were offered. I persuaded them to remain a few days longer, for I was desolate at the thought of parting. The privacy I had so often craved while I was with them was here, behind a door: but now was aching loneliness.

The southern Hejaz 1946

I had no inclination to return to England. I decided instead to go to Jedda and travel in the southern Hejaz mountains and the Assir. For years I had longed to visit this little-known corner of Arabia. During the next three months I travelled there, riding a thousand miles, some by camel, some by donkey, accompanied by a Sharifi boy from the Wadi al Ahsaba. Together we wandered through the Tihama, the hot coastal plain that lies between the Red Sea and the mountains, passing through villages of wattle and daub huts reminiscent of Africa. The people here were pleasantly easy and informal in their manners. We watched them, dressed in loincloths and with circlets of scented herbs upon their flowing hair, dancing in the moonlight to the quickening rhythm of the drums, at the annual festivals when the young men were circumcised. We stayed with the Bani Hilal, destitute descendants of that most famous of all Arab tribes, in their mat shelters on the lava fields near Birk; and with the nearly naked Qahtan who bear the name of that ancestor who sired the Arab race, and live today in the gorges of the Wadi Baish. We visited weekly markets, which sprang up at dawn in remote valleys in the mountains or packed for a day the streets of some small town. We saw towns of many sorts: Qizan (or Jizan), Sabyia, Abha and Taif. We climbed steep passes where baboons barked at us from the cliffs and lammergeyer sailed out over the misty depths, and we rested beside cold streams in forests of juniper and wild olive. There were wild flowers here, jasmine and honeysuckle, roses, pinks and primulas. Sometimes we spent the night in a castle with an Amir, sometimes in a mud cabin with a slave, and everywhere we were well received. We fed well and slept in comfort, but I could not forget the desert and the challenge of the Sands.

cf. pp. 69, 72, 73, 74

cf. pp. 70, 75
cf. p. 68
cf. pp. 71, 74

First crossing of the Empty Quarter 1946

At last I went back to London and reported to Dr Uvarov, head of the Locust Research Centre. I was able to assure him that the floods from the coastal ranges seldom reached the Sands; that in consequence there was no permanent vegetation to afford an 'outbreak centre' for locusts in the Sands between Mughshin and the Hadhramaut. Pleased with this information Dr Uvarov said to me, 'I wish you could get into the interior of Oman. That is the country that really interests us. Unfortunately the Sultan won't hear of your going there.' 'Get permission for me to go back to Mughshin', I replied, 'but don't for God's sake mention Oman.' We discussed this for a long time and at last Dr Uvarov agreed. As I left his office I thought triumphantly, 'Now I shall be able to cross the Empty Quarter'.

The Bait Kathir were waiting for me in Salala when I returned in October 1946, twenty-four of them, most of whom had been with me the year before, including their head sheikh, Tamtaim, a delightful old man, still active in spite of his years; Musallim bin Tafl, who had proved a redoubtable hunter and kept us in meat; and Sultan, the dominant personality in the tribe. I found one of the Rashid in the town and sent him with a message to bin Kabina and certain others of his people to join me at Shisur.

We were watering at Shisur when the sentry gave the alarm. We hurriedly couched our camels. In the distance riders were approaching. We fired two shots over their heads, whereupon one of them dismounted and threw up sand into the air. As they drew nearer someone said, 'They are Rashid. I can recognise bin Shuas's camel'. There were seven and we formed up in a line to receive them. They halted their camels thirty yards away, couched them, and came forward, carrying their rifles over their shoulders; only bin Kabina was unarmed. When they were a few yards away Mahsin, whom I identified by his lame leg, called out, 'Salam alaikum' (Peace be on you), and we answered together, 'Alaikum as salam' (On you be peace). Then, one behind the other, they passed along our line greeting each of us with the triple nose kiss. They then formed up opposite us. Tamtaim said to me, 'Ask their news', but I answered, 'No, you do so. You are the oldest.' Tamtaim called out, 'Your news?' Mahsin answered, 'The news is good'. Again Tamtaim asked, 'Is anyone dead? Is anyone gone?' Back came the immediate answer, 'No, don't say such a thing'. More questions and answers, which never varied. Then they unsaddled their camels while we made coffee and set out dates. When they had joined us the youngest of our party poured coffee, a few drops in the bottom of a small cup, and handed it to Mahsin and the others in order of their importance. Now at last we would get the real news. They sat before us, very unhurried in their movements, quiet and slow of speech, careful of their dignity in front of strangers. Only their dark watchful eyes flickered to and fro, missing nothing.

Mahsin sat with his crippled leg stiffly out in front of him. He was a compactly built man of middle age with a square face. His thin lips were pinched and there were deep lines round his mouth and nose. I knew that before he was wounded he had been famous as a raider and had killed many men. But Muhammad al Auf interested me most, for the Rashid had talked of him the year before. He looked about thirty-five years old. He was famous for his journeyings and his knowledge cf. p. 78 of the desert. He had a fine face, skin and flesh moulded over strong bone; his eyes, set wide apart, were flecked with gold, while his nose was straight and short, his mouth generous. His hair, long and wavy, was unbraided and fell about his shoulders. When we got up bin Kabina came over and joined me. 'How are you, Umbarak?' he asked, using the name by which the Arabs knew me. I was delighted to see him. He was in rags, but in my saddlebag was a new shirt, a loincloth and a dagger which I had brought him. I had six spare Service rifles with me and one of these I lent him.

We left Shisur on 9th November in the chill of dawn; the sun was on the desert's rim, a red ball without heat. We walked until it got warm, then one by one, as the inclination took us, climbed up the camels' shoulders and settled in our seats for the long hours ahead. The Arabs sang, 'the full-throated roaring of the tribes'; the shuffling camels quickened their pace, thrusting forward across the hard ground, for we were on the steppes which border on the Sands. We noticed the stale tracks of oryx, saw gazelle bounding stiff-legged across the plain, and flushed occasional hares from withered bushes in shallow watercourses. In the late afternoon of the second day we saw the Sands, a shimmering rose-coloured wall stretching across our front, intangible as a mirage. The Arabs, roused from the nodding torpor of weary, empty hours, pointed with their sticks, shouted and broke into a sudden spate of talk. We camped that night among some *ghaf*, large mimosa-like trees. Deep down the questing roots had found water, and their branches were heavy with flowering trailing fronds that fell to the clean sand.

I had told the Rashid that I wished to cross the Sands. Bin Kabina said at once, 'Al Auf can get us across'. The other Rashid agreed to accompany us, and Sultan and Musallim bin Tafl asked to come with us. We agreed that the rest of our party should go and wait for us near the coast at Bai.

cf. p. 78

Eight days after leaving Shisur we reached Mughshin. As we approached the well the camels unaccountably panicked, scattering in great plunging bounds. When I looked back Mahsin lay crumpled on the ground. We ran to him. His damaged leg was twisted under him and he was moaning faintly. We tried to straighten him, but he screamed. I fetched morphia from my saddlebag, gave him an injection and then we carried him on a blanket to the trees. We fashioned rough splints from branches and set his leg, all splintered bone. His nephew bin Shuas crouched beside him, keeping the flies off his face, while the others sat round him discussing whether he would live or die. Then we rose and set about our tasks, watering the camels and cooking food.

It now seemed that this accident would frustrate my plans, since the Rashid declared that they must all remain with Mahsin till he recovered or died, for he had many blood feuds on his hands and if his enemies heard the news they would come far to kill him. Sultan was already suggesting that instead of trying to cross the Empty Quarter we should hunt oryx to the east. However, after further discussion among themselves the Rashid agreed that al Auf and bin Kabina should go with me. I now told Sultan that I would send bin Kabina to fetch more Rashid if none of the Bait Kathir wished to cross the Sands. Eventually he agreed that provided we took eight other Bait Kathir he and Musallim would come. I argued in favour of a smaller party with only the best camels, but he was adamant. He said the Al bu Falah of Abu Dhabi and the Bin Maktum of Dubai were at war, and tribes beyond the Sands were involved, and in any case the Duru, through whose territory we must pass on our return, were hostile.

We had left Salala with ample rations, but my companions, after leaving some with their families, had with their customary improvidence used up most of what remained. We now divided what we had, between the thirteen of us crossing the Sands, the Rashid staying with Mahsin, and Tamtaim's party going to Bai. Our share was about two hundred pounds of flour, enough rice for two meals, a few handfuls of maize, some onions and a little butter, coffee, tea and sugar. This must last at least a month. It worked out at half a pound of flour a day for each of us. We were going to be very hungry. I reckoned that we could probably carry enough water for twenty days if we rationed ourselves to a quart a day. Twenty waterless days was the very most that camels could stand, travelling for long hours across the Sands, and they would only do that if we found grazing. Should we find grazing? That is the question that always faces the Bedu. They maintain that in cold weather they can survive for as long as seven days without food or water. It is the collapse of their camels that haunts them. If this happens death is certain.

We had been at Mughshin for nine days. Mahsin was better. For several days he had not eaten, but now he was feeding again and he said the pain was less. Bin Shuas would be able to shoot gazelle, of which there were a number in the vicinity, and one of the camels was in milk. That night we camped a few miles from the well. At last I had started on my journey across the Empty Quarter.

I joined al Auf, who was herding the camels, and we sat together in the twilight and talked of the journey ahead. He had crossed the eastern Sands two years before. He told me he was worried about the condition of some of the Bait Kathir camels. He doubted if they would be able to cross the Uruq al Shaiba, which he described as mountains of sand. I asked if we could avoid them, but he said they extended a week's journey to the west and ended in the east against the Umm al Samim, those legendary quicksands of which Bertram Thomas had heard the Bedu speak. Cross the Uruq al Shaiba we must, he said, if we were to reach Dhafara and the oasis of Liwa. I had heard the Bait Kathir use the expression 'As far as Dhafara' to describe the limit of the world. I had never heard of Liwa where, according to al Auf, the palm groves and villages extended for two days' march. This oasis must be far bigger than Jabrin, discovered by Cheesman in 1924. There were fascinating discoveries to be made in the desert ahead if we could only get there. As I stood up to go back to camp al Auf said, 'There are Bait Musan ahead of us. With them we will exchange the worst of our camels. Don't worry, Umbarak. God willing we will reach Liwa.'

At first we rode through country familiar to me from the year before. Isolated dunes, two or three hundred feet high, rose in apparent confusion from the desert floor. Each dune was known individually to the Bedu, for each had its own shape that did not vary perceptibly over the years, but all had certain features in common. On the north side of each dune the sand fell away from beneath the summit in an unbroken wall, at as steep an angle as the grains of sand would lie. On either side of this face sharp-crested ridges swept down in undulating curves, and behind there were alternating ridges and troughs, smaller and more involved as they got further from the main face. The surface was marked with diminutive cf. pp. 80–81 ripples, of which the ridges were built from the heavier and darker sand, while the hollows were of smaller paler-coloured grains. It was the blending of these colours that gave such depth and richness to the sand: gold with silver, orange with cream, brick-red with white, burnt-brown with pink, yellow with grey. There was an infinite variety of colours and shades.

Four days after leaving Mughshin we reached Khaur bin Atarit, discovered by some forgotten Bedu but still bearing his name. The well was drifted in, but we dug it out. The water, as I expected, was very brackish and would get worse the longer it remained in the goatskins. Musallim made porridge for our evening meal, the only meal of the day. From now on we should be eating gritty lumps of unleavened bread smeared with a little butter. Bin Kabina poured water over our outstretched hands. This was the last time we should wash, even our hands, until we reached the wells at Dhafara.

In the morning we gave the camels another drink. Several refused to touch the bitter-tasting water, so we held up their heads and poured it down their throats. We filled the skins and plugged the tiny dribbling holes. The others said their midday prayers; then we loaded the camels and led them away between the golden dunes. We went on foot, for the full skins were heavy on their backs. The next morning we found a little parched herbage on the flank of a high dune and let our camels graze for two hours. Where we camped the dunes were very big, whale-backed massifs rising above white plains of powdery gypsum. The scene was bleak and cheerless, curiously arctic in appearance. Twice I woke in the night and each time Sultan was brooding over the fire. We started again at sunrise and four hours later came to large red dunes, close together, covered with green plants, the result of heavy rain two years before. Fresh camel tracks showed that the Bait Musan were camped nearby: Sultan and the Bait Kathir went off to find them. Bin Kabina warned me that the Bait Kathir were going to make trouble.

When they came back Sultan informed me that, as our camels were in poor condition and the Bait Musan said there was no grazing ahead, it would be madness to go on. Anyway we were short of food and water. The Bait Kathir were prepared to travel with me in the Sands to the east before rejoining the others near the coast. They would on no account try to cross the Empty Quarter. I asked al Auf if he would come with me and he said quietly, 'We have come here to go to Dhafara. If you want to go on I will guide you.' I asked bin Kabina and he answered that where I went he would go. I knew Musallim was jealous of Sultan. When I asked him he said, 'I will come', whereupon his kinsman Mabkhaut volunteered to join us. The others said nothing. Once again we divided up the food. We took our share, fifty pounds of flour, some of the butter and coffee, what remained of the sugar and tea, and a few dried onions. We also took four skins of water, choosing those that did not leak. Later, after much haggling and for an exorbitant price, we bought a spare camel from the Bait Musan, a large, very powerful bull. Our other camels were all females. That evening I told my four companions that I was giving them as a present the Service rifles with which I had armed them. I watched the disbelief slowly fade from bin Kabina's eyes. He had confided to me that he intended to buy a rifle with the money I would give him. No doubt he had visualised himself the proud owner of some ancient weapon, such as he had borrowed when he accompanied me to the Hadhramaut. Now he cf. p. 76 had one of the finest rifles in his tribe, with fifty rounds of ammunition.

Next morning the Bait Kathir helped us load our camels; we said goodbye, picked up our rifles and set off. The Rashid took the lead, their faded brown clothes harmonising with the sand: al Auf a lean, neat figure, very upright; bin Kabina more loosely built, striding beside him. The two Bait Kathir followed close behind with the spare camel tied to Musallim's saddle. Their clothes, which had once been white, had become neutral-coloured from long use. Mabkhaut was the same build as al Auf, whom he resembled in many ways, though he was a less forceful character. Musallim, compactly built, slightly bow-legged and physically tough, was of a different breed. The least attractive of my companions, his character had suffered from too frequent sojourns in Muscat and Salala.

The sands here were covered with yellow-flowering tribulus, heliotrope and a cf. p. 77 species of sedge. In the Sands, even in areas that have been barren for years, vegetation will spring up after rain and if the rain has been really heavy it may remain green, without even a further shower, for as long as four years. After two hours we encountered a small boy, dressed in the remnants of a loincloth, herding camels. He was from the Rashid and led us to a camp nearby. Here three men sat round the embers of a fire. They had no tent; their only possessions were saddles, ropes, bowls and empty goatskins, and their weapons. Bedu such as these, having located grazing, which is often very hard to find, move on to it in the autumn. They remain there, sometimes a hundred miles from the nearest well, for six or seven months until the weather becomes hot. They live on camel's milk, which suffices them for food and drink, the camels obtaining sufficient moisture from the green plants. On grazing such as this camels can last months without a drink of water.

These men were very cheerful and full of life. The grazing was good; their camels, several in milk, would soon be fat. Life by their standards would be easy this year, but tonight they would sleep naked on the freezing sand, covered only with their flimsy loincloths. There were other years, such as al Auf had that very morning described to me, when the exhausted men rode back to the wells, to speak through blackened, bleeding lips of desolation in the Sands, of emptiness such as I had seen on the way here from Mughshin; when the last withered plants were gone and walking skeletons of men and beasts sank down to die. I thought of the bitter wells in the furnace heat of summer when hour by reeling hour men watered thirsty, thrusting camels, till at last the wells ran dry and importunate camels moaned for water that was not there. I thought how desperately hard were the lives of the Bedu in this weary land, how gallant and enduring was their spirit. The milk they gave us at sunset was soothing, in contrast to the bitter water which had rasped our throats. In the morning they handed us a small goatskin full of milk to take with us.

I noticed, as we were preparing to leave, that bin Kabina no longer wore his loincloth under his shirt. I asked him where it was and he said, 'One of them asked me for it'. I told him that he could not travel without a loincloth through the inhabited country beyond the Sands, and gave him some money to give the man instead. He protested, 'What use will money be to him here? He needs a loin-cloth.' 'So do you', I answered, and grumbling he retrieved it. Our hosts bade us go in peace and we wished them the safe-keeping of God. There were no more Arabs ahead of us until we reached Dhafara.

At first the dunes were separate mountains of brick-red sand, rising above ash-white gypsum flats ringed with the vivid green of salt-bushes. Later they were even higher – five hundred feet or more – and honey-coloured. At sunset al Auf doled out to each of us a pint of water mixed with milk, our ration for the day. After we had eaten the bread that Musallim cooked, bin Kabina took the small brass coffee-pot from the fire and served us with a few drops each. We piled more wood upon the fire, long snake-like roots of tribulus, warmed ourselves for a while and then lay down to sleep. A chill wind blew in gusts, charged with a spray of sand. I was happy in the company of these men who had chosen to come with me; I felt affection for them personally, and sympathy with their way of life. But though the easy equality of our relationship satisfied me, I did not delude myself that I could be one of them. Nevertheless I was their companion, and an inviolable bond united us, as sacred as the bond between host and guest, transcending loyalties of tribe and family. Because I was their companion on the road they would fight even against their own tribesmen in my defence, and would expect me to do the same. But I knew that for me the hardest test would be to live with them in harmony and not to let impatience master me; neither to withdraw into myself, nor to become critical of standards and ways of life different from my own.

Next morning we found a small patch of grazing and for an hour or two let our camels graze. Before going on we collected bundles of tribulus to feed to them in the evening. We were worried about our water: all the skins were sweating and there had been a regular ominous drip from them throughout the day. There was nothing we could do but press on, yet to push the camels too hard would founder them. They were already showing signs of thirst. After we had fed, al Auf decided we must go on again. We rode for hours along a salt flat. The dunes on either side, colourless in the moonlight, seemed higher by night than by day. Eventually we halted, and numbly I dismounted. I would have given much for a hot drink, but I knew I must wait eighteen hours for that. We lit a fire, warmed ourselves and lay down. I found it difficult to sleep. I was tired; for days I had ridden long hours upon a rough camel, my body racked by its uneven gait. I suppose I was weak from hunger, for even by Bedu standards the food we ate was a starvation ration. But my thirst troubled me most. I was always conscious of it.

The others were awake at first light, anxious to push on. In a few minutes we were ready. We plodded along in silence. My eyes watered with the cold; the jagged salt-crusts cut and stung my feet. The world was grey and dreary. Then gradually the peaks ahead stood out against a paling sky; almost imperceptibly they began to glow, borrowing the colours of the sunrise that touched their crests.

A high unbroken dune chain stretched across our front like a mountain range of peaks and connecting passes. Several of the summits seemed at least seven hundred feet above the salt flats on which we stood. The face that confronted us, being on the lee side to the prevailing wind, was very steep. Al Auf told us to wait and went forward to reconnoitre. I watched him climb up a ridge, like a mountaineer struggling upward through soft snow, the only moving thing in all that empty landscape. I thought, 'God, we will never get the camels over that'. Some of them had lain down, an ominous sign. Bin Kabina sat beside me, cleaning the bolt of his rifle. I asked him, 'Will we ever get the camels over those dunes?' He pushed back his hair, looked at them, and said, 'Al Auf will find a way'. Al Auf came back, said 'Come on', and led us forward. It was now that he showed his skill, choosing the slopes up which the camels could climb. Very slowly, a foot at a time, we coaxed the unwilling beasts upward. Above us the rising wind was blowing streamers of sand. At last we reached the top. To my relief I saw we were on the edge of rolling dunes. I thought triumphantly, 'We have made it. We have crossed the Uruq al Shaiba.'

cf. p. 79

We went on, only stopping to feed at sunset. I said cheerfully to al Auf, 'Thank God we are across the Uruq al Shaiba'. He looked at me for a moment and answered, 'If we go well tonight we shall reach them tomorrow'. At first I thought he was joking. It was midnight when at last al Auf said, 'Let's stop here, get some sleep and give the camels a rest. The Uruq al Shaiba are not far away.' In my troubled dreams that night they towered above us, higher than the Himalayas.

Al Auf woke us while it was still dark. The morning star had risen above the dunes and formless things regained their shape in the dim light of dawn.

We were faced by a range as high as the one we had crossed the day before, perhaps even higher, but here the peaks were steeper and more pronounced, many rising to great pinnacles down which the flowing ridges swept like drapery. These sands, paler than those we had crossed, were very soft, cascading round our feet as the camels struggled up the slopes. It took us three hours to cross. From the summit we looked down to a salt flat in another great trough between the mountains. The range on the far side seemed even higher than the one on which we stood, and behind it were others. I thought, 'Our camels will never get up another of these awful dunes'. Yet somehow they did it. Then, utterly exhausted we collapsed. Al Auf gave us a little water to wet our mouths. He said, 'We need this if we are to go on'. I pointed at the ranges ahead but he said, 'I can find a way between those; we need not cross them'. We went on till sunset, but now we were going with the grain of the land, no longer trying to climb the dunes – we could never have crossed another. We fed, got back on our camels and only stopped long after midnight; we started again at dawn.

cf. pp. 82–3, 84–5, 86, 87

In the morning a hare jumped out of a bush: al Auf knocked it over with his stick. By three in the afternoon we could no longer resist stopping to cook it. Mabkhaut suggested, 'Let's roast it in its skin to save water'. Bin Kabina led the chorus of protest: 'No, by God, we don't want Mabkhaut's charred meat. We want soup. Soup and extra bread. We will feed well today. By God, I am hungry.' We were across the Uruq al Shaiba, and intended with this gift from God to celebrate the achievement.

As bin Kabina cooked the hare he looked across at me and said, 'The smell of this meat, Umbarak, makes me feel faint.' They divided the meat and then cast lots for the portions. Bedu generally do this; otherwise there are heated arguments, someone refusing to accept his portion, declaring he has been given more than his share. After we had taken it, bin Kabina said, 'I have forgotten to divide the liver. Give it to Umbarak.' After a show of protesting, I accepted it; I was too hungry to refuse. No Bedu would have done this.

Al Auf told us it would take three more days to reach Khaba well in Dhafara, but that he knew of a very brackish well, nearer; the camels might drink its water. We rode again late into the night and there was a total eclipse of the moon. Again we started very early and rode for seven hours across rolling dunes. The colours of the sands were vivid, varied and unexpected, in places the colour of ground coffee, elsewhere brick-red, purple or a curious golden green.

Here we encountered Hamad bin Hanna, one of the sheikhs of the Rashid. He was looking for a stray camel, but abandoned his search to come with us. He told us that Ibn Saud's tax collectors were in Dhafara, and advised us to avoid contact with the tribes, so that my presence would not get known. I had no desire to be arrested and taken off to explain my presence here to Ibn Jalawi, the formidable Governor of the Hassa. But we must at all costs avoid giving the impression that we were a raiding party, for honest travellers never pass an encampment without seeking news and food. It was going to be very difficult to escape detection. Two days later we were at Khaba well, on the edge of Dhafara. The water here was only slightly brackish, delicious after the filthy, evil-smelling dregs that we had drunk the night before. We had passed another well but even our thirsty camels would not drink the bitter stuff. Here they drank bucketful after leathern bucketful. I have since heard of a test when a thirsty camel drank twenty-seven gallons.

That night bin Kabina made extra coffee and Musallim increased our ration of flour by a mugful. This was wild extravagance, but even so the food he handed us was woefully inadequate to stay our hunger now that our thirst was gone. The moon was high above us when I lay down to sleep. The others talked around the fire, but I closed my mind to the meaning of their words, content to hear only the murmur of their voices, to watch their outline sharp against the moonlit sky, happily conscious that they were there, and beyond them the camels to which we owed our lives.

I had crossed the Empty Quarter. It was fourteen days since we had left the last well at Khaur bin Atarit. To others my journey would have little importance. It would produce nothing except a rather inaccurate map that no-one was ever likely to use. It was a personal experience and the reward had been a drink of clean, tasteless water. I was content with that. This journey was set in the framework of a longer journey, and my mind was already busy with the new problems which our return to Bai presented.

Return from the
first crossing 1946–47

We went north to the outskirts of Liwa, and bin Kabina visited the settlements to buy something for us to eat; I was disappointed not to be able to go there myself. By now we had finished the last scrap of our food and for three days we starved, awaiting his return. I had hoped he would bring back a goat, but all he had been able to buy were dates and a little wheat. Al Auf said disgustedly, 'Soon we shall be too weak to get on our camels'. We had to get back across Arabia, travelling secretly, and we had enough food for ten days if we were economical. The Duru, through whose territory we must pass, would make trouble if they discovered I was a Christian. They owed allegiance to the Imam of Oman, a fanatical reactionary who hated all Europeans. His Governors were in all the big towns, and the Riqaishi in Ibri was reputed to be the worst of them. Yet Ibri was the only place where we could hope to buy food.

Musallim, striking the sand with his camel stick to give emphasis to his words, said, 'Listen, Umbarak, don't hang about in the Duru country and don't go near Ibri. Have you not heard of the Riqaishi? By God, what do you suppose he will do if he knows there is a Christian in his territory? He hates infidels. God help you, Umbarak, if he gets hold of you.' We agreed that we must pass quickly and secretly, but somehow we must get more food from Ibri. The others said, 'We are bound to encounter Duru: how are you going to account for yourself?' I thought and then suggested, 'I will say I am a Syrian from Damascus on my way to visit the Sultan at Muscat'. 'Who are the Syrians?' bin Kabina asked and I answered, 'If you don't know I don't suppose the Duru will either'

Near Rabadh Musallim suddenly jumped off his camel and pulled a hare from a shallow burrow. We stopped to cook it; except for the hare which al Auf had killed, we had not eaten meat for a month. We sat in a hungry circle round the fire. Just as it was ready bin Kabina looked up and said, 'God! Guests!' Three Rashid were coming towards us across the sands. We greeted them, asked the news and made coffee for them, then Musallim dished up the hare and set it before them, saying with every appearance of sincerity that they were our guests, that God had brought them, that today was a blessed day. They asked us to join them, but we refused. When they had finished bin Kabina put a sticky lump of dates in a dish and called us over to feed. Next morning one of them invited us to come to his tent, saying he would kill a camel for us, but as there were many Arabs in the neighbourhood we reluctantly refused. Two days later we came unexpectedly on an encampment. The old Rashid to whom it belonged would brook no refusal. He slaughtered a young camel and for two days we feasted. He had heard of me as the Christian who had travelled with the Rashid to the Hadhramaut the year before, and made me very welcome.

Three days later we were on the eastern edge of the Sands; ahead of us lay Oman. At dawn I saw a great mountain to the east which Musallim told me was Jebel Kaur near Ibri. It was not marked on the map. Later the haze thickened and hid it from our sight. In the nearby Wadi al Ain we encountered a delightful old Duru called Staiyun. He accepted the account I gave of myself and invited me to stay in his encampment, while his son Ali, with al Auf and Mabkhaut, went to buy provisions in Ibri. They were pleasant, lazy days. Staiyun fed us on bread, dates and milk, spending most of his time with us. The more I saw of the old man the more I liked him. The others returned after six days and we were off again. We crossed two more great wadis, that ran down from the Oman mountains and emptied their occasional floods into the Umm al Samim. Perhaps another year I should be able to explore these quicksands; there was no time now. We must get to Bai as quickly as we could if we were to keep our rendezvous.

Each seemingly interminable day dragged on from dawn till sunset. The others ate dates before we started off, but I could no longer face their sticky sweetness and fasted till the evening meal. Hour after hour my camel shuffled forward, seeming to move always up a slight incline towards an indeterminate horizon; nowhere in all that glaring emptiness of gravel plain and colourless sky was anything my eyes could focus on. I watched the sun's slow progress and longed for evening. When at last the sun sank into the haze it was an orange disc without heat or brilliance.

On 31st January 1947 we reached Bai, where the others were waiting for us. We had parted from them at Mughshin on 24th November. We rode back towards Salala across the flatness of the Jiddat al Harasis, long marches of eight and even ten hours a day. I was as glad to be back in their friendly crowd as I had been to escape from it at Mughshin. I delighted in the surging rhythm of this mass of camels, the slapping shuffle of their feet, the shouted talk, the songs that stirred the blood of men and beasts so that they drove forward with quickening pace. Then we climbed from the void of the desert on to the crest of the Qarra range and looked once more on green trees and grass, the beauty of the mountains and the distant sea. We rode singing into Salala, and the Wali feasted us in a tent beside the sea.

Dhaufar to the Hadhramaut 1947

A large gathering of Rashid under bin Kalut, who had taken Bertram Thomas across the Sands, were waiting to go with me to Mukalla. From them we heard that Mahsin had recovered. Among them was a boy with a face of classic beauty; rather sad and pensive in repose, it lit up when he smiled, like a pool touched by the sun. Antinous must have looked like this, I thought, when Hadrian first saw him in the Phrygian woods. Bin Kabina urged me to let him join us, saying he was the best shot in the tribe, as good a hunter as Musallim. 'He is my friend. For my sake let him come with us. The two of us will go with you wherever you desire.' I told him he could come, and handed him one of the spare rifles to use. His name was Salim bin Ghabaisha.

cf. p. 90

A few evenings later bin Kabina stood up to fetch his camels, walked a few paces and collapsed. He was unconscious when I reached him. His pulse was very feeble and his body nearly cold; he was breathing hoarsely. I carried him over to the fire and covered him with blankets. His breathing became easier and his body warmer, but he did not recover consciousness. I sat beside him, hour after hour, wondering miserably if he was going to die. I remembered how I first met him in the Wadi Mitan, how he had joined me at Shisur, remained with me when the Bait Kathir deserted me. I remembered his happiness when I gave him the rifle. I knew that whenever I thought of the past months I should think of him, for we had shared everything, even my doubts and difficulties. Hours later I felt him relax and knew that he was sleeping. By the following afternoon he had fully recovered.

We took a different route from the one we had followed the year before. We had plenty of food, so we fed well and travelled slowly towards our journey's end, which I had no desire to reach. Often bin Ghabaisha came back to camp with an ibex or a gazelle slung over his shoulder, and dropped it triumphantly beside the fire; then we ate the meat for which bin Kabina and I had hungered in the Sands. One evening I saw a young man sitting under a cliff near our camping place. I noticed that his wrists were shackled with a short length of heavy chain. I greeted him but he did not reply, though he turned his head and looked at me. He had a striking face but there was no intelligence in his eyes. His hair was long and matted and the rag he wore did not cover him. He stood up, yawned and walked away. Later I asked bin Kabina who he was and he said, 'He is Salim bin Ghabaisha's brother, the unfortunate one. Three years ago he lost his reason. Before that he was one of the friendliest boys in our tribe.' I asked why he was shackled and he answered, 'Two years ago he killed a boy while he slept; battered in his skull with a rock. The boy was his greatest friend. The family accepted blood money because he was mad. God make it easy for him.'

Bin Ghabaisha returned a little later carrying an ibex he had shot. Bin Kabina told him his brother had turned up; without a word he went off to find him, carrying a dish of dates. Later he came back depressed and unhappy and took me aside. 'Have you any medicine, Umbarak? I beseech you, if you have, to give it to me. I loved my brother; we were inseparable. I was like his shadow. We did everything together, went everywhere together. Now he barely knows me. He wanders round like an animal. By God, today my camel is more responsive. Cure him, Umbarak, and all that I have is yours, only cure him.' There were tears in his eyes as he implored me. I said sadly, 'I have no medicine that will help your brother. Only God can cure him.' He said resignedly, 'God is merciful'.

Accompanying us to Mukalla was a small man with very bright eyes. He looked, I thought, rather like an assertive sparrow, for his movements were quick and jerky. He wore a large silver-hilted dagger set with cornelians, and he was never parted from his brass-bound Martini rifle. I asked bin Kabina who he was. He looked at me in surprise. 'Don't you know him? He is bin Duailan, known as "The Cat". A sheikh of the Manahil.' I looked at him again with interest, for bin Duailan was the most famous raider in Southern Arabia. Eight months later he led a raid which was to plunge the desert into war. Even now the country through
cf. p. 91
which we passed was more disturbed than it had been the year before.

We reached Mukalla on 1st May and here I parted from bin Kabina, bin Ghabaisha and the others, not knowing if I should ever see them again.

Prelude to the second crossing 1947–48

Before going back to England I returned for two months to the southern Hejaz, accompanied by bil Ghaith, a light-hearted young Harbi. I rode once more along the Tihama coast, again watched garlanded men and boys dance throughout the breathless, moonlit night, and stayed with the Amir in the small port of Qizan, sweltering in the heat of summer. We dragged camels up the seemingly impassable face of the escarpment, followed for a while the strange, paved 'Road of the
cf. p. 67, 72
Elephant', and reached Najran in the country of the Yam on the edge of the Empty Quarter. Then we returned to Jedda.

In deserts, however arid, I have never felt homesick for green fields and woods in spring, but now that I was back in England I longed with an ache that was almost physical to be back in Arabia. The Desert Locust Control offered me a job with a good salary and the prospect of permanent employment supervising the destruction of locusts. But this was not enough. I craved the wide emptiness of the Sands, the fascination of unknown country and the company of the Rashid. The western Sands still offered the challenge I sought; to cross them would complete the exploration of the Empty Quarter.

cf, pp. 92–3, 94, 95 I went back to the Hadhramaut and spent the next two months travelling among the Saar. Boscawen in 1931 had hunted on the edge of their country, and Ingrams had paid them a cursory visit in 1934. A large and powerful tribe, they had been aptly described as 'the wolves of the desert'. They had been the most formidable and feared raiders of southern Arabia, but in recent years the Dahm and the Abida from the Yemen had proved themselves more aggressive. Their raids involved two hundred men or more, covered as much as a thousand miles and lasted up to two months.

cf. p. 100 Amair, a hard-faced lad of little charm, joined me while I was among the Saar. He had been with me on two previous journeys. He brought news of bin Kabina, who had received a letter from me on the edge of the Sands, taken it to the coast to have it read, and foundered his camel on the way back, in all a journey of nine hundred miles. He was now on his way to meet me at Manwakh, accompanied by cf. p. 100 Muhammad, his half-brother, son of old bin Kalut. Bin Ghabaisha, Amair told me, was somewhere out of touch near Salala. I suggested sending a wireless message when we returned to Tarim, asking the RAF at Salala to contact bin Ghabaisha through the Wali and fly him to Mukalla. Amair said, 'He is only a boy. I don't think he has ever seen a plane. He might get in one if you were with him; he won't on his own.' However, I sent the message and ten days later bin Ghabaisha turned up in the Hadhramaut. Very erect, his head thrown back, he greeted me in a rather gruff voice, odd in a boy of his age. He wore his dagger and was neatly cf. p. 96 dressed as always. I asked him if he had minded travelling in an aeroplane. 'Why should I mind? You sent for me and so I came.' 'Had you ever seen an aeroplane before?' 'Yes, once, very high up. It made more noise than this one. Where do you wish to go?' I told him. 'I shall need a rifle.' 'Choose one of those', I said, pointing to five Service rifles. Eventually he selected one. 'This is indeed a good rifle, Umbarak.' 'Take it, it is yours, and one hundred rounds of ammunition.' 'With this rifle I can go anywhere!' he said, smiling. Armed with it he was to become in a few years' time one of the most renowned outlaws on the Trucial Coast, with half a dozen blood feuds on his hands. A skilled rider and a deadly shot, he was always graceful in everything he did. He had a quick smile and a gentle manner, but I already suspected that he could be both reckless and ruthless. Amair was equally ruthless, but had none of bin Ghabaisha's charm. He had a thin mouth, hard unsmiling eyes and a calculating spirit without warmth.

We left the Hadhramaut and rode northward to Manwakh, one of the only two permanent wells in the Saar country, an area the size of Yorkshire; it was situated on the edge of the Empty Quarter. In the sharp cold of the winter morning we rode into the Saar camp, passing herds of fat milch camels which the boys had just driven out to graze. Small black goat's-hair tents were scattered along the valley. Naked infants romped round them and dark-clad women sat churning butter, or moved about gathering sticks or herding goats. Several families had struck their tents and loaded their camels. The small children were seated in camel litters, the first I had seen in southern Arabia, though I was familiar with them in the north. These were Maaruf Saar, who for a dozen years had pastured their herds near Najran and acknowledged King Ibn Saud as their overlord, but some of them had been implicated in the recent raids on the Yam so, fearing retribution, the Maaruf had all fled southward to seek refuge among their kinsmen.

Bin Kabina and Muhammad were waiting for me in the Saar camp. Muhammad, heavily built like his father bin Kalut, and already going bald, was an amiable if rather self-important person, the least competent of my four companions. Bin Ghabaisha was probably the most competent and bin Kabina the most endearing.

There were many Saar collected at Manwakh where the talk was all of raids and rumours of raids. A large force of Abida from the Yemen was even then raiding to the east and it was said that they had fought off a pursuit party from the Rashid after suffering some casualties. I already knew that bin Duailan, 'The Cat', had recently surprised two Government posts in the Hadhramaut and captured a number of rifles and much ammunition. I now heard that he had led a large force of Manahil in another raid against the Yam. The raiders had killed ten Yam and captured many camels, but bin Duailan and eight other Manahil had been killed. Bin Duailan had remained behind to give the others time to drive off the looted camels. He had fought to the last before he was knifed. Later I met the man who killed him. He said admiringly, 'By God, he was a man. I thought he would kill us all.' Ibn Saud, infuriated by these raids on his tribes, had given the Yam and Dawasir permission to retaliate on the Mishqas, their collective name for the southern tribes. We now heard that advance parties of Yam were even then ravaging the country to the west of Manwakh, killing anyone they met. In consequence the Saar were preparing to abandon Manwakh. I had arrived only just in time if I was to start from there.

One of the Saar called bin Daisan was reputed to know these western Sands and I was anxious for him to accompany us. I offered him a rifle and a large sum of money, but avarice fought a losing battle with the caution that comes with old age. In the evening he would agree to come with us: in the morning he would go back on his word. We knew we must have at least one of the Saar with us, otherwise their tribe, blood enemies of the Rashid, might follow us into the Sands and kill us. Everyone at Manwakh assured us we should in any case be killed by the Yam or the Dawasir. They said contemptuously that my Rashid were too young and inexperienced to judge the risks ahead of us. Young they certainly were: Muhammad was perhaps twenty-five years old, Amair twenty, bin Kabina and bin Ghabaisha seventeen. Yet they refused to be intimidated or to desert me, though realising far better than I the dangers that faced us. I was more concerned with the physical difficulties of crossing the Sands, especially without a guide, than with the risks we ran from the tribes once we had crossed. Looking back I was to realise how greatly I had underestimated this danger: how very slight had been our chances of survival.

Second crossing of the Empty Quarter 1948

Finally we persuaded two young Saar, called Salih and Sadr, to come with us, in return for a rifle and fifty rounds each. They had watered at the Hassi the year before, and were confident of finding this well once we reached the Aradh, a limestone escarpment that jutted a long way southward into the Sands. I reckoned we had four hundred waterless miles ahead of us before we reached the

Hassi. We watered our camels again in the morning and filled our skins. Muhammad invoked the protection of God and then we started our journey. We had with us four baggage camels and on them we loaded most of the water-skins and the food, of which we had a sufficiency. The water, at least at first, was clean-tasting, unlike the bitter stuff bin Kabina and I had drunk the year before. Later in the day we crossed the tracks of the Abida returning from their raid with a large herd of looted camels.

At first the weather was grey, with a bitter north-east wind. The Sands were flat, drab and desolate; day after day there was no grazing. The camels were already beginning to show signs of distress and I missed the reassuring presence of al Auf. We were travelling in the direction given us by bin Daisan which I hoped was correct. After six days we chanced on a patch of rich grazing. We could easily have missed it, for it was only two or three miles across. It was alive with larks and butterflies and the sand was patterned with the tracks of gerbils and gerboas. Here our camels gorged to repletion. In the next three months they were only to get two more such meals.

Days later we came to the extensive plain of the Jilida which bin Daisan had described, and knew that we were half-way across. Wind-polished fragments of rhyolite, porphyry, jasper and granite formed a mosaic set in hard sand above an underlying conglomerate. We had seen oryx during the preceding days; here we saw a herd of twenty-eight. Two days after leaving the Jilida we were faced by the mountainous dunes of the Bani Maradh. Luckily the easier slopes faced south, but even so they imposed a severe strain on our famished camels, which by now were also very thirsty. One of them collapsed as we struggled over the dunes; to revive her we poured a little of our precious water down her nostrils. These dunes were a lovely golden red; the ones behind us had been dreary and uninspiring.

Beyond the Bani Maradh we found tracks, some less than a week old, of many Arabs and camels. Later we learnt that rain further north had drawn the Yam and Dawasir with their herds out of these Sands and thereby saved our lives. From now on two of us scouted continuously ahead, and each evening before we stopped someone remained behind to watch back along our tracks. We cooked our evening meal before it was dark, put out the fire, and talked in whispers. One night bin Ghabaisha noticed that the camels were watching something. He signed to us; we got into position; and lay with rifles handy through the night. It had begun to rain and was very cold. In the morning we found the tracks of a wolf. 'God! Awake all night in the rain on guard because of a wolf', Muhammad exclaimed disgustedly, and bin Ghabaisha answered shortly, 'Better than waking up with a dagger between your ribs'.

We reached the limestone escarpment of the Aradh. When I woke at dawn the valleys were filled with eddying mist above which the silhouettes of dunes ran eastward like fantastic mountains towards the rising sun. The world was very still, held in a fragile bowl of silence. Standing at last on this far threshold of the Sands, I looked back almost regretfully the way that we had come. I had crossed cf. p. 97 the Empty Quarter for the second time, a journey almost as testing as the first.

Two days later, as we approached the Hassi well, we rounded a corner and came unexpectedly on eight mounted Yam. They were only a few yards from us. I saw bin Ghabaisha slip his safety-catch forward. No-one moved or spoke until I said 'Salam alaikum', and an old man replied. A boy whispered to him, 'Are they Mishqas?' and he snarled back, 'Don't you know the Arab? Don't you know the foe?' I could see the hatred in his eyes. We told them that our main party was just behind and warned them to be careful. I wondered what we would have done if we had surprised them in the Sands. Perhaps if we had taken their rifles and camels we could have let them live. Twenty minutes later we were at the well. It was sixteen days since we had left Manwakh.

Ibn Saud's guardian was not at the well, so Salih and Sadr watered their camels, filled their water-skins, took all they could carry of our rations, and slipped away. A year later on the Trucial Coast, I heard that they had arrived safely. When the guardian returned he took us to Sulaiyil, a small oasis town. He was very hostile when he learnt that I was a Christian, a foretaste of what lay ahead. In Sulaiyil the Amir, who was a young slave, and the two wireless operators, were friendly; everyone else was hostile, hating me as a Christian and my companions because they were Mishqas. The elders spat on the ground whenever they passed, and the children followed me chanting derisively, 'al Nasrani, al Nasrani' – the Christian, the Christian. That evening the Amir said to us, 'By God, you were lucky. Did you not know that Ibn Saud had given his tribes permission to raid the Mishqas? For years raiding has been forbidden. Now they are wild with excitement. Any of them would have killed you if you had run into them. Ten days ago the country to the south was full of our Bedu. Nothing could have saved you, especially if they had found out one of you was a Christian. Even here in the town you can see how they hate you.' I realised how badly I had misjudged our chances, and this increased the responsibility I felt towards my companions who had appreciated the risks and yet come with me.

Sulaiyil to Abu Dhabi 1948

Two days later the Amir received orders from Ibn Saud that we were to be imprisoned, but the next day he received further orders that we were to be released and allowed to continue our journey. St John Philby had fortunately been in Riyadh and been able to intervene with the King on my behalf. We left Sulaiyil next morning on our way to Laila, a hundred and fifty miles away. Abu Dhabi, our destination, was at least six hundred miles beyond that, and none of us knew the country ahead. The townsfolk at Laila were even more fanatical than at Sulaiyil. They reviled my companions for bringing the Christian to their town and made difficulties when we tried to buy food, declaring that our money must be washed. Eventually we obtained a little food, but no-one would guide us to Jabrin. 'Go and die in the desert, don't come back here', they shouted as we left.

Jabrin was a further hundred and fifty miles away according to Philby's map. I believed that I could find the oasis by following a compass bearing. The others, especially Muhammad, were sceptical. 'Crossing the Sands we could not miss the Aradh: a few palm trees are different.' Bin Ghabaisha said, 'God forbid we should stay here'. Bin Kabina agreed and added, 'We must trust Umbarak'. All of us realised that if I went wrong we should be lost in the waterless desert. My diary shows that it took us eight days to reach Jabrin, and that our marching hours were not very long; only twice did we do more than eight hours. But my recollection is of riding interminably through glaring, haze-bound wilderness, without beginning and without end. The weariness of our camels added to my own, making it barely tolerable, especially when their bodies jerked in flinching protest as they trod with their worn soles upon the flints, which strewed alike the hollows and the ridges. After we had halted, hobbled them and turned them loose I suppose they found something to eat during those shuffling quests that took them so far afield. Bin Kabina turned from watching them and said to me, 'Their patience is very wonderful; what other creature is as patient as the camel? That above all is what endears them to us Arabs.'

Eventually I saw in front of us the palm groves, dark against the khaki plain, but the oasis was drought-stricken and there were no Murra here. Between Jabrin and Abu Dhabi the map showed only Dhiby, a well that Thomas had located at the end of his great journey across the Sands. It was another hundred and fifty miles away, and I had a horrid feeling that al Auf had declared its water undrinkable. Now, to add to our hardships, it rained almost continuously for three days and intermittently for the next four, especially heavily at night, the rain soaking away into the sand. We had nothing in which to catch it. Each morning we exchanged the sodden misery of the night for the cold dripping discomfort of the day. Very little food was left from the meagre supply we had secured at Laila. One evening Muhammad grumbled that we must increase our rations. I lost my temper: 'Eat the lot tonight and then at least we shall know where we stand.' The others intervened to quiet us. Day after day there was nothing for the camels. Each morning I expected to find some of them dead. We were in the Jaub depression which I hoped would lead us to the Dhiby well. Those were bad days.

cf. p. 98–9, 100

On the eighth day after leaving Jabrin I got cross bearings on two rocky peaks, shown on the map as near the well. 'We are at the well', I said. Bin Ghabaisha found it nearby. 'By God, Umbarak, you *are* a guide. The very best', he said admiringly. Unfortunately the water was too brackish for us, but the camels drank enormous quantities. Amair said, 'If we get desperate we shall have to push a stick down their throats and drink their vomit'. I knew Bedu were sometimes reduced to doing this. The idea did not appeal to me.

cf. p. 101

Two days later we came on abundant vegetation. Bin Ghabaisha said to me as we watched the camels hasten from plant to plant and rip off great mouthfuls, 'God's bounty. It has saved the camels. They were almost finished, especially those two over there.' Later they lay down and belched and chewed contentedly. 'God's gift', the Arabs call them.

But we were still in trouble; we had very little food and water left. We would never get direct to Abu Dhabi, it was too far. We agreed we must turn back into the Empty Quarter and hope to find Liwa. Bin Kabina thought he would recognise the big dunes where we had camped two years before, and he did. Fifteen days after leaving Jabrin and with only a gallon or so of water left we found a shallow well, brackish but drinkable, and from there bin Kabina took us to the settlements. The Manasir who lived there were the first people we had encountered since the Arabs who had cursed us as we left Laila, more than five hundred miles away. They gave us a guide to take us to Abu Dhabi, yet another hundred and fifty miles ahead. As we approached the sea we slithered across interminable blinding salt flats; we then waded across the creek which separated Abu Dhabi from the mainland, and after a further ten miles of empty desert arrived at a large castle that dominated a small dilapidated town along the seashore. Near the castle were a few palms and a shallow well, where we watered our camels. Then we sat under the castle wall waiting for the sheikhs to wake from their afternoon slumbers. It was 14th March 1948. We had left Manwakh on 6th January.

The Trucial Coast and its hinterland 1948–49

Sheikh Shakhbut received us with great kindness, especially warming after our reception at Sulaiyil and Laila. He showed us to a house on the waterfront and said, 'This is your home for as long as you will stay with us', and here we remained for twenty happy days, thankful that for a while there was no further

cf. p. 102

need for travelling. Once again we ate meat and slept when we felt inclined. The house was always full of friendly visitors. From them bin Kabina and the others could hear the news for which they had craved so long. We spent a few agreeable

cf. p. 106

days with Hiza and Khalid, the Sheikh's brothers, sailing in a small dhow among the islands. Then we rode at leisure across the sands to visit Shakhbut's other brother Zayid, at Muwaiqih. I had heard the Bedu speak of him with admiration.

cf. p. 102

'Zayid is a Bedu, he knows how to ride and fight.'

I hoped to return the following year and explore the interior of Oman. It was now too late in the season and I was too tired. Wellsted had travelled in Oman in 1835. He had been followed by Aucher-Eloy, by Colonel Miles and finally by Sir Percy Cox in 1901. All four of them had travelled in Oman with the approval of the Sultan of Muscat, its effective ruler. Since then the tribes in the interior had thrown off their allegiance to the Sultan and elected an Imam. The present Imam was bitterly opposed to the Sultan and fanatically hostile to all Europeans. Much remained to be examined if I could get there. Jebel Kaur was shown on no map; Jebel al Akhadar was largely unexplored; no European had seen Umm al Samim. As soon as I met Zayid I felt confident that he could and would help me. When I discussed my plans with him he said, 'The tribes, the Duru in particular, will try to stop you. Above all you must not fall into the hands of the Imam. I don't know what he would do to you. Anyway I have friends in Oman and will do what I can to help you.'

Before leaving Muwaiqih I hunted Arabian tahr, a species of wild goat, on a nearby mountain and secured some specimens for the British Museum. I was the first European to have seen this tahr. Then, riding a superb Batina camel which Zayid lent me, I travelled to Dubai. Zayid sent four of his retainers with me since we would pass through the territory of the Bani Kitab who were hostile to the Rashid. In 1948 the sheikhs along the Trucial Coast relied on armed retainers to maintain their position and in time of war sought the support of the tribes. Only the year before the rulers of Abu Dhabi and Dubai had been at war.

cf. p. 103

I stayed for a while in Dubai, then still a fascinating unspoilt Arab seaport, and at the beginning of May sailed on a dhow to Bahrain. Storms drove us to seek shelter off the Persian coast where we were joined by many other *boom* sailing home from Zanzibar. These beautiful craft were almost the last trading vessels in

cf. pp. 104–5, 106, 107

the world to make long voyages entirely by sail.

cf. p. 66

At the end of October 1948 I returned to Muwaiqih accompanied by bin al Kamam, the Rashid sheikh who had been seeking a truce from the Dahm at the time we crossed the western Sands. Bin Kabina and bin Ghabaisha joined us and we spent the next month exploring Liwa oasis, fifty miles of palm groves and settlements scattered among great golden dunes. Close though it was to the coast, no European had yet been there to deprive me of my discovery. Everywhere the Sands were like a garden after the recent rain. Occasional beauty such as this was all the Bedu ever knew of the gentleness of life. Generally bitter winter turned to blazing

cf. pp. 88–9

summer over a parched and lifeless land.

We were back in Muwaiqih in time to go hawking with Zayid at the opening of

cf. p. 111

the season in December. Thirty of us followed him into the Sands, singing the *tagrud* to which the Bedu trot their camels. His falconers each carried on his wrist a hooded peregrine or a saker. For an unforgettable month we ranged the Sands hawking McQueen's bustard, and I watched the contests in the sky enthralled. The falcon, whether peregrine or saker, never waited on, but was flown from the fist. It often saw the bustard on the ground before the Arabs did. As the falcon, flying near the ground, approached, the bustard would take to the air, but it would often land again when overtaken. It would then try to beat off the falcon with blows of its wings, or to squirt at it an evil-smelling fluid. Meanwhile the salukis, which always accompanied us, would have raced off on seeing the falcon take wing. When they arrived, unless the falcon had already fastened to it, they would drive the bustard back into the air. The falcon appeared to fly much faster than the bustard with its slow wing beats, but I once saw a bustard outfly a peregrine after a long hard chase. The peregrine always bound to its quarry when it struck. However the most spectacular display I watched was between a peregrine and a stone-curlew, twisting and turning close over our heads. In the evenings we rode back to camp, with sometimes half a dozen bustards and some hares for our meal.

cf. pp. 108, 109, 110

Inner Oman 1949–50

On 28th January six of us, including bin Kabina and bin al Kamam, slipped away from Muwaiqih. Bin Ghabaisha remained behind to harry the Bani Kitab with whom he had a feud. I was happy to have bin al Kamam with me; a lean middle-aged man, with a quick receptive mind and restless spirit, he was the most widely travelled of the Rashid and the most intelligent, quick to tell me anything he thought might interest me. I carried a letter from Zayid to Yasir, Sheikh of the Junuba, asking him to help me.

cf. p. 113

Detained in the Wadi al Ain by bitter weather, so cold that our camels staled blood, we were confronted by a truculently vociferous gathering of Duru declaring that they would allow no Christian in their land. More and more of them arrived, often two on a camel; fortunately among them were Staiyun and his son, who immediately came over and sat beside me, and thereby split the Duru. 'Umbarak is a good man, I know him; he stayed with me two years ago', the old man asserted. 'Now I will take him wherever he wishes to go, with or without your consent.' His advocacy won the day. I asked him later if on my first visit he had guessed I was a European. 'No. We often wondered who you were, but it never occurred to us you were a Christian.'

He took me down to Umm al Samim, which bordered the Sands for nearly a hundred miles. A tawny plain blended with a dusty sky; the ground at our feet was of gypsum powder, coated with a sand-sprinkled crust of salt. Staiyun put his hand on my arm. 'Don't go any nearer, it is dangerous.' A few dead salt-bushes marked the edge of firm land; beyond them only some darkening of the surface betrayed the bog below. 'I once watched a flock of goats disappear here', Staiyun said. 'Have you not heard of the Awamir raiding party that tried to cross Umm al Samim and was swallowed up?'

Eventually we reached the southern coast near the island of Masira. I had crossed southern Arabia once again. This was the sort of journey to which I was by now accustomed. The journey from here however, back through Oman, was one which would require diplomacy rather than physical endurance.

We visited the Wahiba. A friendly tribe with the bearing of aristocrats, comparable with the Rashid, they were a striking contrast with the uncouth Duru. Two of them led bin Kabina and me northward through the Wahiba sands to the valley of the Batha Badiya, beyond which we could see the stark range of the Hajar. At my request we returned through the settled country of the Sharqiya. 'When we meet Arabs keep silent', they told me. We were still on foot when we met three men and a boy, all armed with rifles, leading a string of camels. We stopped and spoke with them. I watched their dark, gypsy eyes inspecting me, never dwelling on me but missing nothing. 'Who is your companion?' 'A Baluch from Sur; buying slaves and on his way to Nazwa.' This was the first of several such encounters. Standing among them waiting for my identity to be revealed I realised that the fascination of the journey lay not only in seeing this country, but above all in seeing it under *cf. p. 112* these conditions.

Several days later we rejoined the rest of my party whom we had left behind with the Wahiba. Here I met Ali bin Said, a Wahiba sheikh. Among the Bedu a sheikh's authority depended entirely on the force of his personality. First among equals, he had no retainers to enforce his orders. Ali, despite his good-natured face and quiet speech, had unmistakable authority. 'So you have returned safely. You are very welcome. You must be tired for you have travelled far. Remain with us and rest. All the Wahiba are your friends.' When we discussed my plans, he warned me, 'The tribes from the north now know that you are here. They will be on the watch for you.' I told him I had a letter from Zayid to Yasir and he said, 'Yasir may be able to get you through. But I don't know whether you will be able to persuade him. Be sure and come back here if you fail. Anyway I will send my representative with you.'

Yasir, a big heavy man with ill-proportioned features and a large beard streaked with grey, was embarrassed when I met him. He owed allegiance to the Imam but was under an obligation to Zayid. Apparently the Imam had given orders for my arrest. When in 1977 I visited Nazwa I was shown a deep pit inside the fort. 'This is where the Imam intended to keep you', the guardian told me.

Yasir rode to Nazwa, which was nearby, and after a stormy interview persuaded the Imam to let him take me to Muwaiqih. When Yasir rejoined us, the Imam's representative was with him. I expected him to be a sour-faced fanatic, and was agreeably surprised when he proved to be a friendly old man with an obvious sense of humour.

Now I had no further cause for anxiety. I could work openly, taking bearings and photographs. Except for the outline of the Jebel al Akhadar and a few of the larger towns the map was blank. We passed close under the precipice of Jebel Kaur. In the distance I could see the Jebel al Akhadar; it stretched for fifty miles across our front, its face scarred by deep gorges, streaks of purple on a background of pale yellow and misty blue.

We reached Muwaiqih on 6th April 1949. We had ridden some eleven hundred *cf. p. 114* miles since leaving Zayid's fort on 28th January.

I returned again to Muwaiqih in November, anxious to visit the Jebel al Akhadar and if possible to climb it. I believed I might succeed if I could get in touch with Sulaiman bin Hamyar, ruler of the mountain. I had heard that he was free from the narrow fanaticism of most of Oman's townsmen, and was interested in the inventions of the West. He owed allegiance to the Imam, but was anxious to establish his independence and consequently was suspect.

Bin al Kamam had left Muwaiqih when I returned but, among others, bin Kabina and bin Ghabaisha joined me. In the Wadi al Ain we were confronted once again by a crowd of hostile Duru. I had been stung twice in the night by a scorpion, and was still in pain and feeling rather sick. We argued for three days and then bin Ghabaisha said to me, 'It is up to you, Umbarak, but if we stay here we shall have to fight for our lives. They are saying it is as meritorious to kill a Christian as to go on the pilgrimage.'

We turned back into the Sands, made a wide detour and succeeded in getting within twenty miles of the Jebel. I had sent a message ahead to Sulaiman, and he sent word back that he would meet me and take me to Birkat al Mauz at the foot of the mountain. But the hue and cry was out, and before he arrived our camp was surrounded by a hundred or more armed townsmen sent by the Imam. Fortunately some Wahiba and Junuba had joined us, which gave them pause.

Sulaiman, a large man with a sallow complexion and long black beard, arrived next day. He was immaculately dressed and wore a cloak of the finest weave. His dagger was ornamented with gold. He took me inside a small mosque nearby, where we had a long talk. He was anxious for British recognition as the independent ruler of the Jebel al Akhadar, and hoped that I would intervene on his behalf. Extremely ambitious, he struck me as a powerful but rather uncongenial personality. On learning that I had no political standing, he was unwilling to defy the Imam by taking me to the Jebel, but he did undertake to cover my withdrawal. Ten days later, on 6th April 1950, we were back at Muwaiqih.

It was disappointing to have failed. To have climbed the Jebel al Akhadar would have crowned my exploration in Oman. I realised that my journeys in Arabia were over. There was nowhere left where I could travel. The Sultan of Muscat, the Imam, Ibn Saud, even the British officials in Aden and Bahrain, had for their differing reasons closed in on me, resolved to prevent further journeys. I had gone to Arabia just in time to know the spirit of the land and the greatness of the Arabs. Shortly afterwards the life that I had shared with the Bedu had irrevocably disappeared. There are no riding camels in Arabia today, only cars, lorries, aeroplanes and helicopters.

For untold centuries the Bedu lived in the desert; they lived there from choice. The great nomad tribes of the north could have dispossessed at any time the cultivators of Syria or Iraq; bin Kabina or bin Ghabaisha could have settled in the valley of the Hadhramaut. All of them would have scorned this easier life of lesser men. Valuing freedom above all else, they took a fierce pride in the very hardship of their lives, forcing unwilling recognition of their superiority on the townsmen and villagers who feared, hated and affected to despise them. Even today there is no Arab, however sophisticated, who would not proudly claim Bedu lineage. I shall always remember how often I was humbled by my illiterate companions, who possessed in so much greater measure generosity, courage, endurance, patience, good temper and light-hearted gallantry. Among no other people have I felt the same sense of personal inferiority.

cf. pp. 115, 116 Bin Kabina and bin Ghabaisha accompanied me to Dubai, and there we parted. 'Remain in the safe-keeping of God.' 'Go in peace, Umbarak', they replied. As the plane climbed up over the town from the airport at Sharja and swung out to sea, I knew how it felt to go into exile.

In Arab dress, such as I normally wore for my Arabian travels.
This photograph was taken by bin Kabina, in the Empty Quarter. *cf. page 38*

OVERLEAF] My caravan going down into desert country from the Qarra mountains
in Dhaufar, November 1945. *cf. page 38*

A Qarra tribesman, Dhaufar, 1945. The Qarra, living in the mountains
just above Salala, and largely independent of the Sultan of Oman's control,
were of ancient pre-Arab origin and spoke their own language. *cf. page 38*

ABOVE LEFT] Riding camels in southern Arabia: a riding saddle had a basic frame
to which saddlebags and rugs were added. *cf. page 38*

BELOW LEFT] Two boys preparing our typical evening meal.
One is a Rashid, one a member of the related Bait Kathir tribe. *cf. page 39*

LEFT] Musallim bin al Kamam, one of the sheikhs of the Rashid tribe. I first met him in late 1945 on my way to Mughshin, and he accompanied me on various later journeys in the Hadhramaut and Oman. *cf. pages 40, 57–8*

FAR LEFT] Salim bin Kabina, of the Rashid, aged about sixteen, soon after joining me in late 1945. Thereafter he accompanied me on most of my Arabian journeys. *cf. pages 39–40*

BELOW] Bedu whom I met at a well·in the Hadhramaut during my 1946 journey from Salala. *cf. page 40*

RIGHT] A woman of the Yam tribe, photographed near Najran, on the south-western edge of the Empty Quarter: I visited Najran in 1947, approaching it from the Assir side. *cf. page 51*

Tribesmen going to market in the Tihama,
the long strip of low-lying land and foothills
between the Red Sea coast and the inland
mountains
of the Hejaz. *cf. page 41*

LEFT] People of the Bani Malik
in a country market place
in the Assir. *cf. page 41*

The Wadi Baish in flood, flowing down from the mountains of the Assir to the Red Sea. *cf. page 41*

Forested country north of Abha: we passed through this
on our way northward from the Assir to Taif, high in the Hejaz
mountains south-east of Mecca. *cf. page 41*

Yam girls near Najran, aged about
nine and thirteen. *cf. page 51*

RIGHT] A boy of the Bani Malik, one of the tribes
of the Assir region, between the Hejaz proper and
the Yemen. On his head he is wearing a garland
of sweet-scented herbs. *cf. page 41*

LEFT] A woman of one of the tribes of the Assir, walking home from market. *cf. page 41*

RIGHT] A shackled prisoner, who had been arrested by the authorities in the foothills near Sabyia. Such arrests, whether for a criminal offence or to secure hostages for good behaviour, were not uncommon. *cf. page 41*

A cultivator in the hot Tihama coastal plains, near Sabyia in the Assir. *cf. page 41*

RIGHT] An elderly slave from the same area, wearing a hat made of palm fronds. At the time of which I write, slaves, or the descendants of former slaves, invariably of negro extraction, were common in Arabia: though a subject class, some could own property and not a few rose to positions of authority and eminence. *cf. page 41*

ABOVE LEFT] Simple traditional wattle and daub huts, reminiscent of Africa, in Sabyia: these beehive dwellings were characteristic of the old quarter of the town, once the capital of the autonomous Assir, but by 1946 a district headquarters of little importance. *cf. page 41*

CENTRE LEFT] Abha, in the Assir, a small town at 7,500 ft: the town was set around the marketplace, itself dominated by the great bulk of the Amir's fortress-residence in the centre: the core of the castle is a warren of centuries-old chambers and stair-cases. *cf. page 41*

BELOW LEFT] A typical plaster-faced house of the new town of Sabyia, built by the Idrisi dynasty as their capital to replace the older town. However, Sabyia was devastated by Saudi forces in 1933, when they annexed the region; the consequential Saudi-Yemen War of 1934 failed to restore the Assir's autonomy; and Sabyia languished. *cf. page 41*

RIGHT] A characteristic watchtower of the Qahtan tribe, north-east of Abha, built of clay with projecting rings of slates to protect the walls against erosion by rain. It has been speculated that the architectural origin of such towers, now falling into ruin through disuse, may antedate Islam. *cf. page 41*

The great trunk wadi,
Umm al Hait –
'Mother of Life' –
near Mughshin on
our approach to the
Empty Quarter in 1946.
A quarter of a century of
unbroken drought had
brought it to this state.
cf. page 39

Yellow-flowering
tribulus (*zahra*) and
a sedge (*qassis*), growing
in the Sands after rain.
After exceptional rainfall,
when the sand
had been soaked deep,
such vegetation might
survive up to four years
without more water.
cf. page 45

FAR LEFT]
Bin Kabina, 1946:
the rifle I gave him is in
the leather cover
the Rashid use to protect
their weapons against sand.
cf. page 45

RIGHT] In the interior of the Empty Quarter: dunes such as these were up to seven hundred feet high. *cf. page 47*

LEFT] My first crossing of the Empty Quarter, late 1946: Muhammad al Auf, my incomparable Rashid guide, whose skill steered us safely over. He is in the typical riding position of the southern Bedu, maintained even at the trot or gallop. *cf. pages 42–4*

LEFT] Bin Anauf, a boy of the Bait Kathir: he was fifteen, and wore his hair in the curious cock'scomb that showed he was not yet circumcised. He and his father were among the majority of my party, who left me before the actual crossing of the Sands and rejoined me later at Bai. *cf. page 43*

OVERLEAF] A distinctive form of dune known as *qaid*, which I found only in the south-eastern Sands and at Liwa: ripple-surfaced sharp-ridged hills of sand, separate and permanent, they were individually known to the Bedu. *cf. page 44*

Bin Kabina,
some camel-
fodder in his
hands, near
the summit
on the
windward
and easy
side of a
great dune.
The sharp
ridge is
formed by
occasional
winds from
the opposite
direction.
cf. pages 47–8

OVERLEAF]
Our diminished
party, well
into the
Empty Quarter,
early December
1946.
cf. pages 47–8

LEFT]
Leading our
loaded camels down
the soft lee slopes
of a dune.
cf. pages 47–8

CENTRE LEFT]
Bin Kabina leading
two camels: as he walks
he feeds them with
any vegetation found
and picked on the way.
Dunes stretch behind,
blown by the wind
into crescent shape.
cf. pages 47–8

BELOW LEFT]
Riding along
the ridge of
a dune in the
Empty Quarter.
cf. pages 47–8

RIGHT]
The heart of the
great dune barrier
that lay across our route.
In particular, there was
no way of avoiding
the long chain of
mountainous dunes
called Uruq al Shaiba,
previously known
to western travellers
only by repute.
cf. pages 47–8

One of the scattered settlements of the vast Liwa oasis.
In 1946, after crossing the Empty Quarter, I camped near Liwa
but could not enter it because of tribal fighting: it was
1948 before I explored it, the first European to do so.
cf. pages 49, 56, 57

Broken terrain in the Mahra country:
we passed through it on my
journey from Salala to Mukalla,
March to May 1947.
cf. page 51

LEFT] Salim bin Ghabaisha
of the Rashid, aged about
sixteen, in March 1947.
He joined me then for the
journey from Salala to Mukalla,
and stayed with me thereafter.
cf. page 50

OVERLEAF] The ancient Hadhramauti town of Shibam, seen from the wells, December 1947:
the high wall surrounding it was dwarfed by the towering, close-packed buildings inside.
cf. page 52

LEFT]
Shibam:
a mosque
and houses.
While I
was here
I bought
supplies–
dried
shark-meat,
butter,
spices,
saddlebags,
ropes and
water-skins–
for my second
crossing
of the
Empty
Quarter.
cf. page 52

RIGHT]
A street
in Shibam:
in these
silent
alleyways,
under the
sheer walls
of the
houses,
it was
like being
at the
bottom of
a well.
cf. page 52

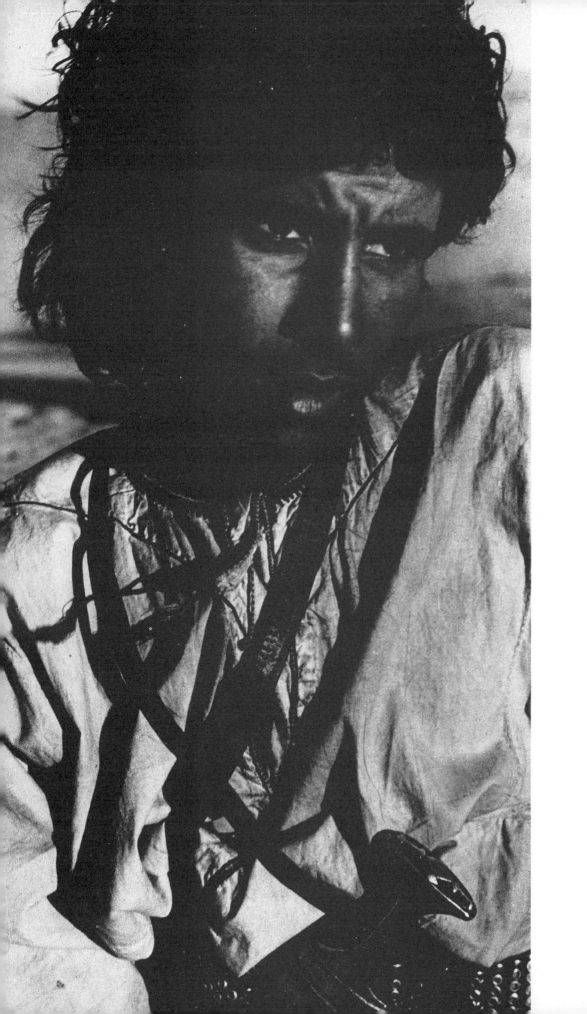

Bin Kabina in the western Sands, 1948. *cf. pages 53–4*

LEFT] Bin Ghabaisha, during the second crossing, from Manwakh to Sulaiyil. *cf. pages 52–3*

OVERLEAF] The desolation of the Sands: travelling eastward from Jabrin in February 1948, on our long march from Sulaiyil to Abu Dhabi. *cf. page 56*

ABOVE LEFT]
A miserable camp-site
in the Jaub,
February 1948:
by now hunger,
thirst and tiredness
were a burden,
and all depended
on finding some
water and grazing.
cf. page 56

BELOW FAR LEFT]
Muhammad bin Kalut
of the Rashid,
who came on my second
crossing in early 1948:
he was half-brother
to bin Kabina.
cf. pages 52–3

BELOW LEFT]
Amair, one of the
four Rashid among
my six companions
during my second
crossing of the
Empty Quarter:
this was one of
three major journeys
he made with me.
cf. pages 52–3

ABOVE RIGHT]
Looking down
from a dune
on Dhiby well:
the five of us
on this journey
from Sulaiyil
had nine camels,
using four for
baggage.
cf. page 56

BELOW RIGHT]
Watering the camels
at Dhiby well,
which we were
lucky to locate:
too brackish
for ourselves,
its water saved
our camels.
cf. page 56

Forts at Buraimi oasis, which was a scatter of settlements
in the hinterland of the Trucial Coast, April 1948. *cf. page 57*

RIGHT] In the traditional *suq*, or market,
at the little seaport
of Dubai, May 1948. *cf. page 57*

BELOW] Sheikh Shakhbut, March 1948, with retainers:
he was Ruler of Abu Dhabi, then a simple village by the sea,
where my journey from Sulaiyil ended. *cf. pages 56–7*

OVERLEAF] An ocean-going *boom*, sailing home to Kuwait from Zanzibar. I photographed it from another *boom*, in which I was travelling from Dubai to Bahrain, May 1949. *cf. page 57*

Launching the small dhow in which I sailed
among the islands off Abu Dhabi, April 1948. *cf. page 57*

RIGHT] Water, brought by sea to Kuwait from the Shatt al Arab river,
being unloaded in goat-skins on to donkeys. I stopped there on my way
to Bushire, in Persia, 1949. *cf. page 57*

BELOW] Hauling up the sail on our *boom*. *cf. page 57*

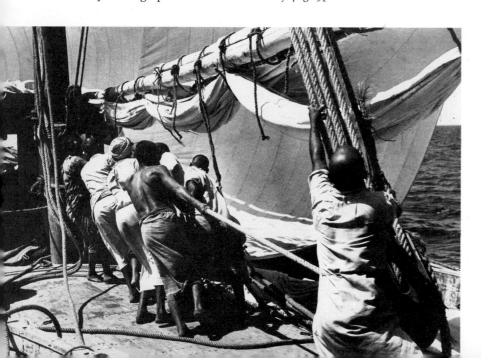

LEFT] Setting out hawking in the morning, accompanied by a saluki: in December 1948
Sheikh Zayid took me hawking for a month, in the Sands south-west of Muwaiqih.
cf. pages 57–8

ABOVE] Peregrines on their block.
cf. pages 57–8

LEFT] A peregrine on a hare it has killed.
cf. pages 57–8

One of Sheikh Zayid's falconers with a peregrine. *cf. pages 57–8*

RIGHT] Sheikh Zayid bin Sultan with one of his hawks near Muwaiqih.
cf. pages 57–8, 298–9

Inner Oman, early 1949: a woman of the Harasis, wearing the
strange visor-like mask of stiff black cloth that their women wore.
cf. pages 57–9

RIGHT] A Junuba from southern Oman: one of various tribesmen who
joined my party in 1949/50 as *rabia*, or companions, whose presence was likely
to guarantee our safety, among their own or certain associated tribes.
cf. page 58

RIGHT] Bin Ghabaisha (*left*) and bin Kabina in Oman in 1950, the year I left Arabia:
twenty-seven years passed, and much had changed, before I met them again. *cf. pages 59–60*

Riding north from Ibri to Muwaiqih, beside the Oman mountains, April 1949;
towards the end of an eleven hundred mile ride in the interior of Oman. *cf. page 59*

Bin Ghabaisha in 1950, aged about twenty, on the Trucial Coast:
he already had a reputation as an outlaw. *cf. pages 59–60*

PERSIA AND KURDISTAN

Iran and Iraq, relating to the chapter on Persia and Kurdistan

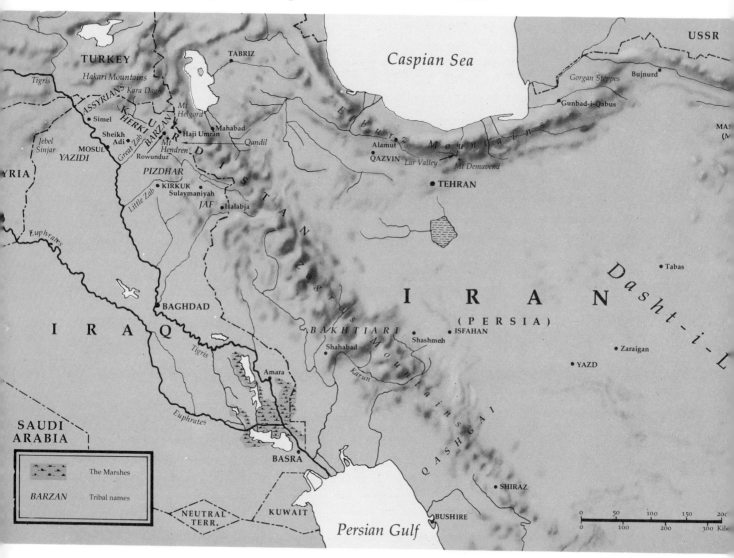

Persia and Kurdistan

Persia 1949–50, 1964

cf. pp. 130–31, 132–3, 134

I first visited Persia in 1949 on my way back to England from Oman, but on that occasion I just passed briefly through the country by car, from Bushire to Shiraz, Isfahan, Tehran and Tabriz, then on through Kurdistan to Baghdad.

The following year I visited Meshed, a city sacred to the Shias because Imam Reza, eighth of the twelve Imams, is buried there. Thanks to the Consul, Norman Darbyshire, a friend of the guardian of the shrine, I was allowed to enter the great mosque, an overwhelming aesthetic experience which had been denied to most European visitors to the town.

I did not return to Persia until June 1964, and then I stayed for six months. I made three long journeys on foot. First I travelled some four hundred and fifty miles through the Elburz mountains from Bujnurd to Alamut. Then, in September, I joined the Bakhtiari tribe on their autumn migration from the Zagros mountains down to the coastal plains. Finally I crossed the Dasht-i-Lut desert from Tabas to Yazd, a distance of over two hundred miles. I was greatly helped by Lew Tamp, a Russian émigré who lived in Tehran and knew Persia intimately. He gave me invaluable advice and took me to the starting point of each journey.

cf. p. 135

Before my first journey I visited with him the Turkoman in their *yurts,* or felt tents, on the Gorgan steppes; I saw the ancient brick-built tower of Gunbad-i-Qabus, which Robert Byron in *The Road to Oxiana* asserted to be finer than the Taj Mahal; and I looked across the Russian frontier at the wire fences and watch-towers, a chilling experience. Then we went to Bujnurd, where I bought two pack mules.

On this journey I was accompanied by a muleteer, and a Kurdish school-teacher who acted as my interpreter. On our first day's march the school-teacher, in poor condition, lagged further and further behind. Eventually I waited for him to catch up. When he did he gasped, 'I am very hot, very thirsty and very tired!' Exasperated, I said, 'I told you it was a long way. We still have more than four hundred miles to go. What is the furthest you have ever walked?' 'From my bedroom to the bathroom, I suppose.' His feet soon blistered so we mounted him on one of the mules which was already heavily laden. But as soon as his blisters were healed he insisted on walking. I found him a good companion, humorous and informative.

Week after week we walked over a bare, tawny land; we crossed wide plains covered with stones, and climbed high wind-swept passes. We sometimes passed the ruins of a castle on a hill-top, or the black tents of shepherd tribes, their sheep standing each with its head in the shade of another sheep's body. Wherever a stream issued from a hillside was a village, with cultivated fields, fruit trees, poplars, walnuts and magnificent *chenar,* the Persian plane trees. But such villages appeared as isolated dots or ribbons of green, in the immense desert setting.

Usually the shepherds were welcoming, but the villagers were almost always churlish and inhospitable. We carried some food with us and paid for anything else. Time and again we hung about on the outskirts of a village, the loads still on our tired mules, while Taj Ali the muleteer tried to find someone who would allow us to sleep on the roof of his house. It annoyed me when the owner invariably turned up to share our meal and eat the chicken for which he had overcharged us, especially as I knew he would demand yet more money for letting us sleep on his roof, or for the oil in the lamp we used. Taj Ali had a heated argument with a man demanding money for the grass the mules had eaten on a hillside near his village. I did not like these people, and this reduced my pleasure in the journey. To me it is always the people rather than the places that matter.

We reached the Lar valley, and spent a few restful days in the Embassy camp, where Sir Denis Wright made us very welcome. There were trout in the river and a view of Demavend, eighteen thousand feet high, framed by the sides of the valley. Then we went on again through bare country even bigger than that through which we had come. We climbed six or seven high passes, coming at last to the final one above Alamut, the Valley of the Assassins. Men were gathering mule-loads of thistles and fennel, all that grew among the rusty red rocks. Around us, and far into the distance, rose great ranges of mountains. In the morning we went down into the valley, through a bank of cloud that emphasised the savage desolation of the scene, to a village perched on a shelf beyond the gorge. Above the village the scant ruins of a castle sat on a fang of rock, accessible only by a precarious path above a two hundred foot drop. From this seemingly impregnable stronghold Hassan-i-Sabbah, the 'Old Man of the Mountains', had ruled his Ismaili sect and despatched his Assassins on their missions of death; there he and his successors had sat like spiders at the centre of their web, for one hundred and seventy years until Hulagu and his Mongols stormed over the pass.

cf. p. 137

Next day we followed the track down the valley, fording the river six times in one mile, and two days later, 2nd September, we arrived at the Qazvin road. We had been travelling for forty-six days.

I was in Tehran for a fortnight before I was given permission to accompany the Bakhtiari on their migration. Both the Bakhtiari and the Qashgai tribes migrate each spring from the low country along the Persian Gulf to the Zagros mountains, where they remain till the autumn before returning to the plains for the winter. They are perhaps the last two tribes who regularly over great distances migrate in a manner unchanged through the centuries. The Bakhtiari nomads numbered about fifty thousand. Both tribes had been virtually independent until Reza Shah ruthlessly curtailed their power in the twenties. Even after that they gave periodic trouble to the Government: consequently it was not easy to get permission to visit them.

cf. p. 136

I hired two mules at a village called Shashmeh to the west of Isfahan, and on 22nd September left there with a muleteer, also a policeman who had been sent with me from Tehran. The main body of the migration was ahead and we hurried to catch up with them, passing many smaller groups. Some of them pitched small black tents when they halted; others were content with shelters of branches. The men wore round black felt caps, sleeveless white coats to their knees with a dark pattern down the back, dark long-sleeved shirts, and very wide trousers. The women wore long, loose dresses, often of red, blue or green velvet, with a kerchief attached to a small cap, hanging down behind almost to the ground. The various families we stopped with were hospitable and friendly. The route they

cf. pp. 138, 139

were following was hard indeed, often a twisting track through and over piles of rock fallen from the precipice above, or along a narrow shelf across a wide *cf. p. 140* limestone face with a sheer drop hundreds of feet below. Sometimes the track *cf. p. 143* crossed and recrossed a river, or climbed through dense oak woods, then went steeply up a bare mountainside to some high pass, where the limestone, polished over the centuries, was slippery as glass. From the passes we looked across successive ranges of the Zagros mountains, their summits high in cloudless skies where ravens tumbled.

After five days we came up with the main body and moved with them, usually camping with a different family each night, having been separated from the previous one during the march. I remember one day that typified the whole migration. Many families had camped the night before near a wood on the lower slopes of a very steep ridge which we had to cross. All around us were the watch-fires. Water was scarce and the flocks and herds were restless. Dogs barked; men shouted at intervals; there was uproar when a wolf attacked a sheep and mauled it. All night I heard the music of the bells, some deep-toned, others of higher pitch, that hung round the necks of sheep and goats; and at intervals the sound of pipes played by shepherd boys. We moved off at half past three, soon after the moon had risen; others had already left. I climbed above the wood and sat beside the track, to watch the migration pass. Below me were the lights of many fires, and from the darkness of the waking valley I heard a rising, falling roar, a flowing river of sound, as the migration moved forward. Flocks of sheep pushed past, their fleeces luminous in the near dark; and separate flocks of black goats, a moving darkness, darker than the hillside. Men and boys passed, pale figures in white coats; and dark, barely discernible women interspersed with scrambling, straining mules and cattle. The light grew stronger. I could disting-uish tents and bedding, pots and pans, sacks of grain loaded on mules and cattle, a puppy on a cow's back, babies in cradles or bundles, carried by the women. Then the birds began to sing in the wood, and the sun came over the mountains. I climbed to the pass; ahead, the track was solid for miles with a thread of slowly *cf. p. 141* moving men and animals.

cf. p. 142 A few days later we came to the ancient shrine at Shahabad, under its curious white cone. Next day we reached the Karun river, and there I left the Bakhtiari.

I was anxious to cross the *Dasht-i-Lut*, or Desert of Lot, before I returned to England. The very name was intriguing. Lew Tamp took me in his Land Rover at the end of October to Tabas, where I hired two camels and a man to look after them. The captain of the gendarmes insisted on sending three of his men with me. When given the order they protested volubly. 'What crime have we committed that you send us into the Dasht-i-Lut?' This was actually much ado about nothing. It took us ten days to reach Yazd and on seven of those days we found water, though sometimes brackish. My own camel was a large baggage camel with a wrenching stride which I soon realised would incapacitate me: I had slipped a disc in my back some years before and was still liable to trouble. I therefore walked upwards of two hundred miles to Yazd. The weather, cool by day, was bitterly *cf. pp. 144–5* cold at night; several times the water-skins froze solid.

We crossed gravel plains and low, bare hills, sometimes gashed by deep watercourses. In places there were drifts of sand, and small salt flats; there was little vegetation except occasional tamarisk bushes. Here we saw four onager or wild ass. They were quite close and although donkeys are unlawful food for

Muslims the gendarmes wanted to shoot them for meat. I deliberately raised my voice in protest; the onager galloped off and the gendarmes sulked. We also saw occasional gazelle and found the skull of a moufflon. Then, after skirting some jagged black mountains we came to the small village of Zaraigan, where there were fruit trees and a little cultivation; and the next day to Shah Kevir, another village of half a dozen houses with a few palms. Beyond this village we marched for ten miles or more across a plain, the surface consisting of salt encrusted with dry mud. Finally we reached an extensive gravel plain with mountains on either side, and arrived at Yazd.

This journey had been a slog through dull country. It lacked the sense of comradeship, of hardship or of danger which would have made it rewarding. Nonetheless I had reached my goal, and the effort of reaching it enhanced for me the significance of Yazd, an ancient Muslim city, still relatively remote and unchanged.

cf. pp. 146, 147

Yazd exceeded my expectation. Of all the Persian cities that I visited it ranks second only to Isfahan, which I saw in 1949 when there were horse-cabs in the streets. I was lucky in Yazd, for there I met Derek Hill, an authority on Islamic architecture, whose company greatly increased my appreciation of the mosques. I had seen what I wanted of Persia, and left it now without regret.

Iraqi Kurdistan 1949–51

After my drive across Persia in 1949, I felt an uplift of the spirit as we climbed over the pass at Haji Umran, into Iraq. Whereas too many Persian Kurds looked down-at-heel in ill-fitting European clothes, the Kurds here wore the finery of tribal dress and carried rifles. It always amazes me when nationalistic governments, many of them hostile to the West, impose upon their subjects European dress, the most unbecoming garb yet invented. I remember my sense of outrage in the thirties when, crossing the Taurus mountains by train, I saw a band of nomads with their camels: one man wore a tattered dinner jacket, another a lounge suit and top hat, in keeping with sartorial innovations decreed by Kamal Ataturk. Baghdad in 1949 struck me as drab, mud-coloured, uninteresting, only redeemed by its river; but over the next nine years it grew on me, and I shall always be grateful to the régime for allowing me freedom of movement unusual in the bureaucratic world of the fifties.

I returned to Iraqi Kurdistan for three months in August 1950 and for another five the following May. I suspect that no foreigner ever saw as much of this country as I did during those eight months; there can have been few villages I did not visit, few mountains I did not climb.

I was accompanied by a cheerful, good-natured and indefatigable young Kurd called Nasser, who spoke Arabic. I knew no Kurdish: only a few of the chiefs, or Aghas, spoke Arabic. Sometimes we hired a mule or a horse to carry our saddle-bags, while we walked; at other times our hosts lent us horses to our next destination, and then we rode. I took little with me: some spare clothes, a few medicines, a book or two – *Lord Jim* and *Kim* have been stand-bys on many of my journeys – a camera, a Rigby .275, cartridges and a couple of blankets in case we camped out. We relied on our hosts for food and bedding. More welcoming and hospitable than Persian villagers, they would have felt insulted if we had fed ourselves. Mostly we ate flaps of unleavened bread with curds, or boiled wheat, sometimes meat and vegetable stews with rice. In season there was fruit: mulberries, apricots, peaches, melons, sometimes grapes.

cf. p. 158

Never had I seen such country: the great rock-girt bastion of Hendren, above the gorge of Rowunduz; Helgord's twelve thousand feet; the snow-capped range of Qandil, with sheer-faced precipices of five thousand feet; and, higher still, across the Turkish frontier, Kara Dagh, the 'Black Mountain', and beyond that the other Hakari peaks. Everywhere one range was superimposed upon another. The knees of the mountains, and the valley sides up to six thousand feet, were wooded with holly-oaks interspersed with a few ash, hawthorn and wild pear, and rare stands of juniper. In the valley bottoms the Zab, the Little Zab and other smaller rivers and torrents flowed down to join the far-off Tigris, foaming ice-cold through narrow gorges of polished rock, and swirling among great boulders tumbled from the cliffs above; or calm in deep green pools under grassy banks and overhanging willows.

In spring there were the wild flowers: red and white anemones on the lower slopes, covering whole hillsides with carpets of colour; and among them red ranunculus like poppies, yellow marigolds, gladioli, stocks, dark blue squills and irises. High up on the mountains scarlet tulips grew in profusion, scattered tiger-lilies flowered in hollows among the rocks, dark blue gentians bordered drifts of snow.

In such a setting the Kurds in tasselled turbans were fittingly colourful. The Jaf, who lived in the south round Halabja and had been nomadic till Persia closed the frontier, wore long robes like the Arabs, with short jackets over elaborately-wound cummerbunds, and baggy trousers drawn in at the ankle. The northern Kurds, the nomadic Herki in particular, wore loose wide-bottomed trousers and tucked their jackets under their cummerbunds. Whereas the Jaf wore dark uniform colours, the clothes of the northern tribes were dyed with blues, greens and browns of varying shades, woven with wide, light-coloured stripes and patterns. Most men were hung about with bandoliers, wore formidable daggers

cf. pp. 151, 156

in their cummerbunds and carried revolvers in holsters at their sides.

The Kurds, generally regarded as the descendants of the Medes, have inhabited at least since Parthian times the mountains where they now live. Today their land is divided between Turkey, Persia and Iraq, while a few live in northern Syria. Formidable fighters and turbulent by nature, their unquenchable craving for independence has led them time and again to revolt against their alien rulers. The Turks, with characteristic brutality, have suppressed them, denied them their identity and the use of their language, and would have them known as Mountain Turks. Reza Shah tried to do the same with the Kurds in Persia: equally harsh, he was less effective. Indeed after the Second World War the Kurds, with Russian encouragement, set up a short-lived Independent Kurdish Republic at Mahabad. The Iraqi Government allowed the Kurds to carry arms, to wear their tribal dress, to learn Kurdish in their schools, and employed Kurdish officials to administer them: yet even these concessions could not satisfy Kurdish aspirations.

The most interesting character I met in Kurdistan was Sheikh Mahmud. Intensely ambitious and aspiring to rule an independent Kurdistan, he had led his tribesmen in insurrection after insurrection from 1919 to 1930 against the British who then controlled Iraq. Defeated each time after fierce fighting, he would be exiled, pardoned and allowed to return, only to rebel once more. His last uprising was against the Iraqis in 1941. I had known him well by repute: some of my older friends, including Guy Moore, who had often spoken of him as we sat beside the fire at Kutum, had fought against him. A stout, jovial figure, Sheikh Mahmud entertained me in his house: in the evening, after we had fed, he would recall ancient battles, and British officers he had known. A few years later he died. I am glad I met him.

cf. p. 157

Another Kurd who caused the Government much trouble was the megalomaniac Sheikh Ahmed of the Barzan tribe. He had been implicated in Sheikh Mahmud's rising in 1919. In 1928 he proclaimed that he was God and instructed a Mullah, whom he declared to be his prophet, to substitute their names for Allah and Muhammad in the call to prayer. Three years later he announced that he was a Christian and ordered his people to eat pork. The neighbouring Baradost tribe, appalled at his blasphemies, attacked him; the Barzan remained loyal, defeated the Baradost and routed a Government force that was sent against them. As the result of bombing by the RAF Sheikh Ahmed was driven across the Persian frontier. After the Second World War his brother Mullah Mustafa rebelled and won several notable victories over the Iraqi forces before going off to Mahabad in Persia to help establish the Independent Kurdish Republic. Deprived of his leadership, the Barzan were defeated and many were deported. When I visited their country most of the villages were ruined and their orchards destroyed. Years later Mullah Mustafa was to return and fight another war against the Iraqi Government, that only ended in 1975 when the Shah ceased to back the Iraqi Kurds. Of all the Kurdish tribes I liked the Barzan best.

cf. pp. 148–9

Nasser and I stayed in villages of flat-roofed houses rising in tiers up the hillsides, and slept in rooms furnished only with rugs and pillows; we shared the black tents, and cabins built from branches, in which the tribes lived in spring after they had moved with their herds to the mountainsides. I remember coming down from Helgord, tired and thirsty, to the tents of the Baliki pitched on green turf where yellow buttercups and pink primulas flowered among the moss, bordering threads of water and shallow pools. How good the yoghurt they gave me tasted.

cf. p. 156

When I was travelling near Sulaymaniyah the Administrative Officer insisted on sending three policemen with me for a two-day journey through the area of a notorious outlaw, Kula Piza. Once a law-abiding man, he had originally been arrested for some minor offence, but after brutal treatment from the policeman, had killed him and taken to the hills. More police were sent after him: he killed them too. Actively supported only by his brothers and a few friends, he made war on the police, killing any he met. He was reported to have accounted for a hundred. He and his band also killed the District Judge from Sulaymaniyah. I should have felt safer without my escort. Kula Piza was eventually killed by the army while I was in northern Kurdistan. The day news of his death arrived official flags were at half-mast for King Abdullah's assassination. Many Kurds, including Nasser, presumed this was a mark of respect for Kula Piza: in their eyes he was a national hero who for years almost single-handed fought the police, local representatives of an Arab Government in Baghdad.

cf. p. 150

That autumn Nasser and I joined the Herki, as they moved down from the high mountains along the Turkish border towards the plains round Mosul. Though the flocks were travelling separately the passes and tracks were choked with loaded mules and ponies. On some of the loads were partridges in wicker-work cages. The women, who wore turbans round soft red caps like fezzes, often carried rifles, which looked incongruous but left the men freer to struggle with wedged animals and slipping loads. The migration covered six or seven miles a day. In the afternoons the tents went up and food was cooked; we stayed with the Agha, Sidi Khan, and fed well. All night there was bedlam as packs of dogs rushed barking from one end of the camp to the other. Great savage brutes, these dogs could be very dangerous to a stranger who approached tents where there were no men to beat them off.

I climbed innumerable mountain faces looking for bear and ibex while in Kurdistan. On one occasion I slipped crossing a tongue of frozen snow and slid for thirty yards or more down the icy slope towards a precipice. Luckily the gradient eased and I clawed to a stop. After that I aways wore felt-soled Kurdish slippers, the best footwear on such mountains. Without the urge to hunt I should never have seen half the country that I did, nor looked on many a stupendous view. But in all my months in Kurdistan I only shot one bear and one ibex, and as I looked on the dead bear I resolved I would never shoot another animal unless for food or because of the destruction it caused. On several of those hunts I was accompanied by a tireless Assyrian, a former officer of the Iraq Levies. He was well-informed about the wildlife of the mountains. During our hunts we sometimes camped in the woods or slept in caves. One night we were woken by the 'woof' of a bear which found us in possession of its home. Bears were not uncommon, especially in the north, but I saw only four. Sometimes we spotted ibex, threading their way across the face of a sheer precipice without apparent footholds – we would sit and watch them while griffon vultures circled above us or a lammergeyer sailed past on motionless wings, so close that I could see the bristles that gave it its other name, bearded vulture; and always there were choughs, swooping and tumbling shrill-voiced around the crags. Not infrequently we disturbed wild boar in the woods, and once I saw a roe deer. Wolves were fairly common and took a toll from the flocks, and in the remoter areas there were said to be some leopard.

cf. p. 159

The Assyrians, who were Nestorian Christians, were an ill-fated people. Their homelands had been in the Hakari mountains, but in the First World War they rose unsuccessfully against the Turks. Some twenty thousand escaped retribution and after a nightmare journey reached Persia. From there they were moved by the British to Iraq, where many were enlisted in the Levies. After Iraq became independent the Assyrians provoked trouble, fought against the army and were defeated. Their defeat was followed by a shameful massacre of their women and children at Simel. Staying near the Hakari mountains in villages which had always belonged to them, I saw what a splendid people they once had been.

cf. p. 156

Another oppressed people whom I met were the Yazidis. Of Kurdish stock, they lived in villages round Jebel Sinjar, a mountain in the desert west of Mosul, and among the Kurdish foothills north-east of Mosul, near the shrine of Sheikh Adi, founder of their community. Reputed to worship the Devil, they were abhorred in consequence by their neighbours and by the Government. I met a senior Kurdish official who was administering them. I had known and liked him when he was in Halabja; now he horrified me by bursting out, 'These filthy people should be exterminated!' In fact the Yazidis do not worship the Devil but seek to placate him, believing that the Supreme Being delegated power to him over the world after he was cast forth from Heaven. They will never say his name, 'Shaitan', nor use any word that begins with 'Sh'. They have various other curious prohibitions: they will never wear blue, nor a shirt opening down the front, nor eat lettuces, nor defecate into water. Their religion, in origin an Islamic dervish brotherhood, now apparently contains elements of nature worship,

Zoroastrianism and Christianity, in which Malek Taus, the Peacock King, has an important place. Once a year, early in October, they assemble at Sheikh Adi and sacrifice a bull to the sun. On the doorway of the shrine is an embossed black serpent, symbol of Shaitan, which the pilgrims kiss. I attended this festival but did not see the sacrifice. Booths had been set up among the trees, near the shrine with its two fluted, pointed white cones, and the scene resembled a fair, crowded with happy, relaxed people. There was much dancing and singing, in which the women joined.

cf. pp. 152, 153, 154–5

The Yazidis round Sheikh Adi affected Kurdish dress; those who lived round Jebel Sinjar wore their own distinctive and becoming garb. The young men and boys, many of whom were remarkably good-looking, dressed in long white shirts and coats, and their braided hair fell in plaits to their shoulders from beneath round felt caps. The older men, of the ascetic order of *Faqirs*, wore short coarse black shirts next to their skin, black turbans round their felt caps, short white jackets and baggy trousers. Most had distinguished faces, enhanced by their long beards. I was captivated by these much maligned people; I had visited most of their villages on the lower slopes of Jebel Sinjar before attending the festival at Sheikh Adi. I would willingly have stayed longer among them, but time pressed.

Nasser and I went south again, travelling hither and thither for some four hundred miles throughout the length of Kurdistan, passing once more through the territories of the Baradost, Mungur, Pizdhar, Jaf and other tribes whom we had already met. Then, far to the south, we left the mountains and reached the plains where Kurd merged into Arab, and here we found ourselves among the Bani Lam, one of the great shepherd tribes of southern Iraq. Escorted by our hosts and riding on their horses, we travelled from one encampment to the next until we came at last to the town of Amara, and beyond it to the strange remote world of the Marshes.

Isfahan, Persia: the *Maidan-i-Shah*, the main square, a third of a mile long, created by Shah Abbas the Great after he made Isfahan his capital in 1598. In 1949 a *doroshkeh*, or horse-cab, was still a regular sight. *cf. page 121*

OVERLEAF] Part of the *Pol-i-Khaju*, a bridge spanning the Zaindeh Rud, the river of Isfahan.
It was built by Shah Abbas II in the middle of the 17th century. *cf. page 121*

RIGHT] The immense and unique brick tomb-tower at Gunbad-i-Qabus, a town on the Gorgan steppes of north-east Persia. Some two hundred feet high, it was built in 1006 as the repository for the coffin of Qabus, a local prince, who died in 1012. *cf. page 121*

One of the domes of the *Masjid-i-Jumeh*, the Friday Mosque or main congregational mosque, at Isfahan. This vast and ancient mosque, though reflecting many architectural periods in its structure, dates substantially from the 11th century. *cf. page 121*

RIGHT] The site of the Castle at Alamut, above the Valley of the Assassins.
It had belonged to the 'Old Man of the Mountains' who captured it in about 1090,
and it was eventually destroyed in 1256 by Hulagu the Mongol. *cf. page 122*

Shepherds' tents on the southern slopes of the Elburz mountains.
The Bakhtiari tents were very similar. 1964. *cf. pages 122–3*

The Bakhtiari. For three weeks I travelled with them, on their autumn migration from the Zagros mountains of western Persia down to the plains. I then left them and made my way to the Dasht-i-Lut. *cf. pages 122–3*

Coming down one of the valleys. Tens of thousands of Bakhtiari made the journey. *cf. pages 122–3*

LEFT] The autumn migration. They migrated back again each spring. *cf. pages 122–3*

OVERLEAF] The *Dasht-i-Lut*, or Desert of Lot, which I crossed in 1964 from Tabas to Yazd, a distance of some two hundred miles. Tabas is the town which was devastated by the appalling Persian earthquake of 1978. *cf. pages 123–4*

RIGHT] Holly-oak and high mountains: the country through which the migration passed. *cf. pages 122–3*

The Imamzadeh, or mausoleum-shrine, of Yaqub ibn Layth, at Shahabad, near the end of the migration. *cf. page 123*

LEFT] Inside the beautifully preserved 14th-century *Masjid-i-Jumeh*, or Friday Mosque, at Yazd. *cf. page 124*

The desert town of Yazd, a centre of Persia's ancient Zoroastrian community,
with distinctive mud-brick architecture: seen from the Friday Mosque. *cf. page 124*

A typical mud-roofed village in the mountains of Iraqi Kurdistan.
After a brief visit in 1949, I spent months travelling in this region in 1950 and 1951. *cf. page 126*

Kurdish horsemen: these two were of the Pizdhar tribe,
one of the many tribes of Kurdish descent. *cf. page 125*

LEFT] The Herki, a migrant tribe of northern Kurdish stock,
on the move from the mountains on the Turkish frontier
down to the plains round Mosul in Iraq. *cf. pages 126–7*

Yazidis in Jebel Sinjar.
The old man, with his distinctive
black shirt, belongs to the Faqirs,
one of the ascetic religious orders
in the Yazidi tribe. *cf. pages 127–8*

Sheikh Adi's tomb,
north-east of Mosul
in the foothills of the
Kurdish mountains:
to this holy place
the Yazidis make their
annual pilgrimage
in October.
cf. pages 127–8

ABOVE LEFT] A small herd-boy from the Baliki tribe. *cf. page 126*

ABOVE] An Assyrian in tribal dress.
A few of these Nestorian Christians, remnant
of the once powerful Assyrian Church and people,
later much persecuted, still cling to part of their
ancient homeland in northern Iraq. *cf. page 127*

BELOW LEFT] A Pizdhar tribesman wearing
bandoliers as they always did. *cf. page 125*

RIGHT] Sheikh Mahmud, one of the great
Kurdish leaders. From 1919–30 he fought
periodically against the British, and later against
the Iraqis, trying to establish an independent
Kurdistan. *cf. pages 125–6*

RIGHT] A Kurdish tribesman hunting bear on Helgord,
the highest mountain in Iraqi Kurdistan. *cf. page 127*

The Qandil range in Iraqi Kurdistan, rising to some 11,000 ft.
In the foreground is Nasser, the Arabic-speaking Kurd
who accompanied me throughout. May 1951. *cf. pages 124–5*

THE MARSHES

The Marshes of Iraq

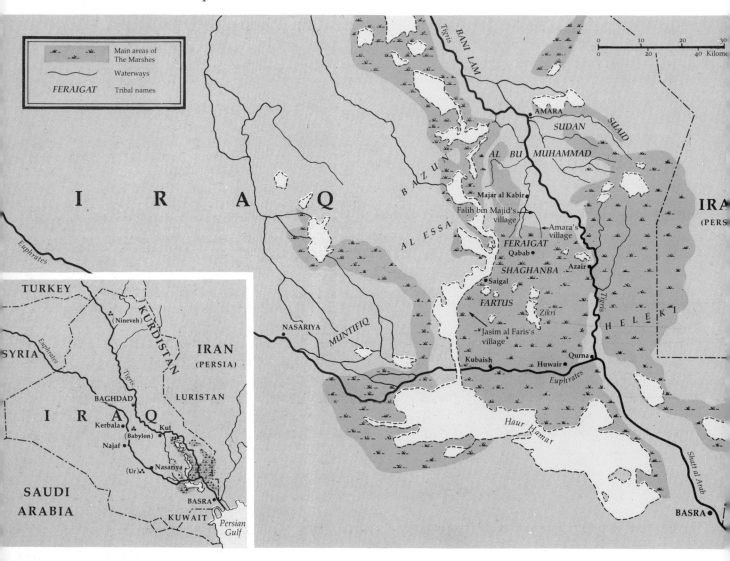

Legend:
- Main areas of The Marshes
- Waterways
- *FERAIGAT* — Tribal names

0 10 20 30
0   20   40 Kilome

Inset map labels:

TURKEY

(Nineveh)

KURDISTAN

SYRIA

IRAN (PERSIA)

Euphrates

Tigris

BAGHDAD

LURISTAN

IRAQ

Kerbala

(Babylon)

Kut

Najaf

(Ur)

Nasariya

SAUDI ARABIA

BASRA

KUWAIT

Persian Gulf

Main map labels:

I R A Q

Euphrates

BANI LAM

SUAID

AMARA

SUDAN

AL BU MUHAMMAD

BAZUN

Majar al Kabir

Falih bin Majid's village

Amara's village

AL ESSA

FERAIGAT

Qabab

Azair

SHAGHANBA

Saigal

FARTUS

Zikri

HELEKI

Jasim al Faris's village

Tigris

NASARIYA

MUNTIFIQ

Kubaish

Qurna

Huwair

Euphrates

IRAN (PERSIA)

Haur Hamar

Shatt al Arab

BASRA

The Marshes 1950–58

First visit to the Marshes of southern Iraq 1950

I went to the Marshes of Iraq almost by chance, in that autumn of 1950. Having spent the summer in Kurdistan I decided to visit the Marshes on my way back to England, principally to see the wildfowl that congregated there in vast numbers at that time of year.

With Dugald Stewart, the Vice-Consul at Amara, I rode across a dusty plain to the black tents of the Bazun. There we watched the flocks being driven in at sunset, each flock moving in a golden aura of dust. Throughout that night their bleating made a background of sound, against which the barking of the dogs rose and fell. Then once again we rode across an interminable plain.

cf. pp. 176–7

We arrived in the dark at the guest tent of Maziad, Sheikh of the Al Essa, another of the shepherd tribes. We slept that night in a cabin built of reeds. The wind blew cold off dark water and I heard waves lapping on an unseen shore.

As I came out at dawn I saw, far away across a great sheet of water, the silhouette of the reed-beds. Nearby was beached a slim, dark, high-prowed craft: the Sheikh's war canoe, waiting to take us into the Marshes. Before the palaces of Ur were built men had stepped out from such a house and launched canoes like this to go hunting in the reeds. Woolley unearthed their dwellings and models of their boats, buried deep under the relics of Sumeria. Five thousand years of history were here, the pattern of life little changed.

That morning I had no idea what I should find beyond those distant reed-beds. We were pressed for time, unable to linger, but even so I gained an impression of a delightful and unexpected world: of narrow waterways winding through the tufted reeds, duck circling above still lagoons, the crying of geese, a village of reed houses clustered on the water, a hum of voices, and the incessant passage of canoes; dark dripping buffaloes, the sun crimson through the smoke of burning reed-beds, a boy's voice singing in the dark, firelight on a half-turned face, the croaking of frogs, and stillness, the stillness of a world that never heard an engine.

Falih bin Majid's mudhif *1951*

Inevitably I returned, and four months later, in February 1951, I stepped ashore from a small leaking canoe paddled by two Arabs, at Falih bin Majid's *mudhif* or guest house. On the bank near the guest house, an impressive barrel-vaulted building roofed with overlapping mats of a pale golden colour, several men were standing. I called out the conventional salutation and they replied. Then one held out a strong hand and heaved me up the bank. 'Welcome; be pleased to enter and make yourself at home.' That was how I met Falih. I kicked off my shoes and passed into the *mudhif* between pillars eight feet in girth, each formed by a bundle of giant reeds, the peeled stems bound so tightly together that the surface was smooth and polished.

cf. pp. 180, 200

The great hall, dim after the bright sunlight, smelt acrid with smoke. Shadowy figures stood along the walls. Again I called out, '*Salam alaikum*', and together they replied, *'Alaikum as salam'*. Falih led me to the far end where we seated ourselves on rugs. This *mudhif*, sixty feet long, twenty wide and eighteen high, gave the impression of far greater size. It was constructed entirely from the stems of a species of reed which grew to more than twenty-four feet in height. The ribbed roof was darkened by smoke to a deep chestnut, as if varnished.

Falih asked the conventional questions about my health and journey, then lapsed into silence. Between an Arab host and his guest long periods of silence are never embarrassing. Meanwhile an old man in a long white shirt, the only person other than myself not wearing a cloak, busied himself among the coffee pots, a dozen of them, the largest two feet high, ranged beside the hearth. He pounded, roasted and brewed fresh coffee beans, and when the coffee was ready poured a few drops into a small china bowl and offered it to Falih, who told him to serve me first. I in turn refused, but when Falih insisted I drank, while the old man poured a second cup for him. After accepting the customary three cups I shook the cup slightly to signify that I had had enough. The coffee man moved slowly round the room serving the others.

cf. p. 200

Falih was the eldest surviving son of Majid, one of the two Paramount Sheikhs of the Al bu Muhammad, a tribe that numbered twenty-five thousand fighting men. He had a powerful virile face, clean-shaven except for a close-clipped moustache, with dark bushy eyebrows that nearly met over a prominent fleshy nose. In his *mudhif* he kept up the state becoming a sheikh of his importance, but later I was to find that among his villagers he was friendly and informal. The warmth with which they greeted him was touching. Children would scamper ahead shouting, 'Falih is coming', and their parents would press him to honour their houses. On occasion he could be hard, even merciless, but no-one ever questioned his judgments. He fulfilled their ideal of a sheikh; nobly born, a leader to admire and trust.

While I studied the men opposite me, contrasting their broad and rather heavy faces with the fine-drawn Bedu features to which I was accustomed, Falih dealt with a succession of cases. Eventually, supervised by Falih's son Abd al Wahid, several servants laid in front of us a circular mat woven of rushes, five feet across. On this they arranged a round tray heaped with rice, dishes of vegetable stew, three roast chickens, a grilled fish, dates, bowls of buttermilk and jugs of sherbet. We washed our hands, ate, and washed again before returning to our places and being served once more with coffee.

Falih asked about my plans and I told him I wanted to go into the Marshes and visit the Madan, the collective name by which the tribes in there were known. 'That is easy. I will send you to Qabab where my father has a representative. Stay there for a while and then come back here.' I thanked him but explained that I hoped to spend several months among the Madan. 'But the Madan live like their buffaloes', he expostulated. 'Their houses are half under water and full of mosquitoes and fleas, and they have no proper food. No, come back here where I can make you comfortable. This house is yours for as long as you will stay with us. From here you can spend the days in the Marshes.' I explained that I had already been there and seen the conditions. I added, 'I am used to hardship. I spent five years in the Empty Quarter, always hungry and thirsty; in the Marshes I shall at least have plenty of water.' Falih laughed. 'Yes, you will sleep in it. Well, if you insist I will tell Sadam at Qabab to send you wherever you wish to go. But don't forget this is your home. You English are a strange people.'

Two days later Falih sent me to Qabab in a canoe paddled by three men. We passed a village that straggled along the river bank, a drift of grey smoke showing above the houses. Children, and women, none of them veiled, watched us in silence; dogs raced along the banks above us, stopping every fifteen to twenty yards to bark at us in a sort of gibbering frenzy. Each group of dogs handed us over at its boundary to a fresh lot. Buffaloes, black sullen-looking brutes, heavy-bodied and shaggy-coated, stood among the houses or rested in the water. Canoes of various size were moored along the banks. We passed fields of wheat and barley, another village, mud flats where some cattle egrets showed up very white, then beds of bulrushes. The water deepened and the canoe-men, laying down the poles with which they had been punting, took up their paddles again.

cf. pp. 178-9

Leaving the muddy flow of the river's mouth behind us among the battered grey bulrushes, we entered the reed-beds of *qasab* (*Phragmites communis*) which covered most of the perennial marsh. This giant grass, which looked like a bamboo, grew densely: the stems, each topped by a tasselled head, were so stout that the marshmen used them as punt poles. In early spring the reed-beds bordering the narrow waterways were light and airy. Relics of the past year, they were pale gold and silvery grey; the new growth at their base, still only a few feet high, was very green.

cf. pp. 192, 196, 197

We passed villagers cutting young reeds as fodder for their buffaloes. In the bows of a canoe stood a naked boy, cutting the green shoots with a saw-edged sickle, then piling them dripping wet behind him. Beyond the curtain of the reeds I could hear talk and laughter. A boy's voice, very clear and true, sang a lilting song. The song ended and someone called out, 'Give us another, Hasan'.

The scene became familiar during the next six years. Sometimes the setting was winter, the water icy-cold under a chill wind sweeping across the Marshes from the far-off snows of Luristan. Sometimes it was summer, the air heavy with moisture, the tunnels at the bottom of the dark towering reeds where mosquitoes danced in hovering clouds, unbearably hot. It seldom seemed to be spring or autumn, brief periods in this part of the world. But whether winter or summer I always associate the reed-beds, where the Marshmen toiled to gather fodder for their insatiable buffaloes, with the sounds of laughter and song.

We paddled down a gradually broadening lane and found ourselves on the edge of a small lake, three-quarters of a mile across. The water was a vivid blue in the sunlight. One of the canoe-men said, 'We will go straight across; there is no wind'. A large band of coot rested on the water and a flock of duck, disturbed by our approach, circled overhead. Back in the reed-beds we overtook canoes loaded with reed-shoots, on their way back to Qabab.

We rounded a promontory of rushes and there, on a shining expanse, just rippled by the breeze, was the village, the houses reflected in the water. A haze of white smoke merged into the pale blue sky above them and a wall of yellow rushes lay beyond. Scattered about the lagoon were sixty-seven houses. From a distance they appeared to be actually in the water but each was in fact constructed on a soggy pile of rushes like a giant swan's nest, just large enough for the building and a space in front where the buffaloes rested at night. The houses, like those on the mainland, were of mats fastened over a framework of *usab*. The newer ones were the colour of fresh straw but most had weathered to a dirty grey.

cf. pp. 183, 184, 194, 195

Everywhere people climbed in and out of canoes to get from one house to another. Sadam's *mudhif* was the largest building in the village and the only one on dry ground, being built on a small island, evidently an ancient site, for brickwork showed near the water-level. Sadam, a tall lean man with a lightly pock-marked face, received me cordially. After we had fed, the canoe-men rose to leave. 'What? You are going? Nonsense, spend the night.' 'No, we have work to do, we must get back.' 'I beg you to stay.' 'No, really we must go. Remain in the safe-keeping of God.' Sadam said, 'All right; go in peace'. And I added, 'Give my salutations to Falih'.

That evening, back in Sadam's *mudhif* after visiting the village, I watched the sun go down behind reed-beds that stretched to the world's end. High overhead banks of cirrus cloud, blown to tattered streamers, ranged from ebony to flaming gold and the colour of old ivory against a background of vermilion, orange, violet and palest green. From all around, as if the Marshes breathed, came the massed voices of frogs, an all-pervading pulse of sound, so sustained that the mind soon ceased to take note of it. More than any other, even than the crying of geese in winter, this was the sound of the Marshes. A dog barked; a buffalo grunted; a man called out a long and to me unintelligible message; a pause, and someone answered. Buffaloes swam across the open water towards the village, only their heads showing, each leaving a wake. A boy, late back from the reed-beds, paddled down a waterway, a path of shining gold leading to the setting sun. He sang softly as he came towards me, the notes lingering in the air. Sadam called and I went inside.

cf. pp. 193, 204–5, 206, 207, 210–11

The Madan marshmen and their ancestry

The Madan were Muslims of the Shia persuasion; they spoke their own dialect of Arabic, and all claimed descent from Arab tribes. In fact their ancestors had been here long before the Arabs came. Far back in the darkness of time, somewhere about the fifth millennium BC, a people already socially and culturally advanced moved down into the Euphrates delta from Iran. They built reed houses, made boats, and harpooned and netted fish. They lived there as men do today, in an environment that has changed but little. Later they were absorbed or displaced by another race from Anatolia who brought with them the domestic buffalo, a knowledge of metalwork, and the art of writing. Then about 3,000 BC the Flood covered the face of the land. But men survived and the Sumerians founded their cities on the site of ancient villages buried under feet of silt.

The centuries passed. Babylon rose and Sumer fell. In 728 BC the terrible Assyrians razed Babylon to the ground. In time, worn out by war and conquest, they were overthrown by the Medes. Nineveh fell. Babylon rose again under the Chaldeans, and flourished until Cyrus gave Nebuchadnezzar's Hanging Gardens to the flames. Other races had invaded Iraq during this same two thousand years: the wild, lawless Gutti who devastated Sumer; the Cassites and the Hittites; the Mittanians, bringing with them strange gods from India; and the people of Elam.

For the next thousand years Persians, Greeks, Seleucids, Parthians, Romans and then again Persians marched their armies across the land, seeking to hold it or wrest it from others.

When, at the beginning of the seventh century AD, the Arabs surged out of the desert on a wave of conquest and overran Iraq, they added another name to the long list of alien conquerors. They, in their turn, founded the Abbasid Caliphate which lasted for five hundred years, sinking from the glories of its early reigns to the chaos of later times. The last of its Caliphs was executed after Hulagu and his Mongols captured Baghdad, his death adding but one more body to eight hundred thousand butchered when they sacked the city. In 1401 Baghdad was sacked again, this time by Timur-leng, last of the great Mongol conquerors; if the slaughter was less it was because there were fewer people in the city. After him came the Turkomans, first the White Sheep and then the Black, and after them the Persians, to be followed in 1534 by the Turks, who held the country until driven out by the British in the First World War.

For thousands of years Iraq, despite these wars and invasions, had been a land of towns and stable agriculture, but the Mongols destroyed the work of centuries, and the irrigation system on which the prosperity of the country depended was irreparably damaged. The country reverted to desert, and Arab nomads from beyond the Euphrates grazed their herds on mounds that had once been the palaces of kings. The desert Arabs who migrated into Iraq were few compared with the indigenous inhabitants, but theirs were the customs and standards that prevailed. When I heard old men sitting round the fire telling legendary tales of courage and generosity, it was not of Cyrus or two-horned Alexander that they spoke, nor of the Caliphs who once ruled in splendour in Baghdad, but of tattered horsemen of the Bani Hilal from the deserts of Arabia.

The Marshes afforded refuge to remnants of defeated people and were from earliest times a centre of lawlessness and rebellion. The blood of the many races that for thousands of years had occupied Iraq may well have survived in this baffling maze of reed-beds. But the ideal which governed the Madan's life, and shaped their whole pattern of behaviour from their blood-feuds to their table manners, was the code of the desert Arabs.

When I went there the Madan had a bad reputation among Arabs and Englishmen alike, a legacy I suspect from the First World War, when from the shelter of their Marshes they murdered and looted both sides indiscriminately. During the few years that the British administered Iraq the Political Officers had been too busy with more urgent matters to concern themselves much with the Madan. Several had travelled repeatedly in the Marshes, but their visits seldom lasted more than a few days. As for Iraqi officials, I felt certain that none of them had been further into the Marshes than was absolutely necessary. Even Falih had said, 'One night in the Marshes is enough for me, when I have to go there on the Sheikh's business.' I was probably the first outsider with both the inclination and the opportunity to live among the Madan.

The world in which the Madan lived covered only about six thousand square miles. Its heart was the almost impenetrable reed-beds, and the extensive lakes such as Haur Hamar and Zikri, dreaded for their sudden storms. Outside this was the seasonal marsh of bulrushes which dried in autumn and winter, and around this large areas of desert which were inundated only during the floods after the snows had melted in the Kurdish mountains. During the phenomenal floods of 1954 I revisited the tents of the Bazun, travelling by canoe across country where four years before Dugald Stewart and I had ridden on horses.

I had spent years in exploration but now there were few untouched places left to explore, at least in countries that interested me. I therefore felt inclined to settle among a people of my choosing. In Arabia I had been very close to my companions, but constant journeying had prevented my knowing any particular community as well as I would have wished. I hoped that here among the Madan I should find what I sought. Their way of life was unique, and the Marshes were beautiful. Here, thank God, was no sign of that drab modernity with its uniform of second-hand European clothes, which was spreading like a blight across so much of the world.

Anxious though I was to be more than a spectator, to be accepted by the people and to share their lives, their not unnatural suspicion kept me at first at a distance. 'Why does he come here? What does he want?' Even Sadam had assumed that I was employed by the Government, and when I denied this asked who paid for my journeys; plainly he disbelieved me when I said that I paid. 'I have travelled in many countries, in the land of the Habash, in the Sudan and Arabia,' I told him, adding, 'I seek knowledge.' Obviously he would not believe me if I said I travelled for pleasure. 'Do you seek knowledge among the Madan?' he asked, looking sceptical. 'Knowledge is to be found in all places', was my sententious reply.

Acceptance by the Madan 1951–53

Each village fed me and sent me on next day to the next. At first I could sense that though I should afford a topic for conversation for some time to come they were glad to be rid of me. Rather depressed, I arrived among the Fartus, where I landed at the tumbledown *mudhif* of Jasim al Faris. Jasim was a Madan sheikh who lived here in the heart of the Marshes in the same manner as his fellow tribesmen. No richer than many of them, his authority stemmed from his personality and to some extent his lineage. He was an elderly man with a deeply lined face, a firm mouth and kindly eyes. He gave me a generous welcome and pressed me to stay.

cf. pp. 185, 186, 190

Accepted by the Fartus I was in due course accepted by the other tribes.

In the evenings we fed on rice soaked in buffalo's milk, a chicken, or duck if I had shot any, and perhaps a fish served with circular loaves of bread. Then Jasim would get busy among the coffee pots on the hearth, where pieces of supposedly dry buffalo dung smouldered, filling the room with bitter smoke. 'Where is Khayal?' Someone would be sent to fetch him. Others too would arrive to a chorus of '*Salam alaikum*', '*Alaikum as salam*'. Falih, Jasim's son, would pick up a drum and tap out a rhythm with his fingertips. 'Come on Khayal, sing, sing', and Khayal, after the customary protests, sang. He was about fourteen, the same age as Falih. Some of his songs were lilting and gay, others mournful. Drawn by the sounds, others paddled over from their houses and soon the room, already crowded, was packed. A small space was cleared and two thin, impish-looking boys were dragged forward and told to dance. They were brothers, the elder about thirteen. Khayal and Falih played the drums, two others banged tambourines.

At first the brothers circled slowly and languidly, their bodies swaying and their arms raised, elbows level with their shoulders. As the rhythm quickened their bodies swung lower, twisted and squirmed, and their feet moved quicker, forwards, sideways, backwards. Everyone was singing now without restraint. The dance reached its climax; suddenly the boys stood, feet apart, their bodies jerking forwards and backwards in ever-quickening thrusts from the hips. The thrusts slowed, their bodies shuddered, as each twitching muscle passed the spasm on to the next. Then, quite casually, the boys stopped, grinned at their audience and sat down. But they were not allowed to remain seated. Again and again they repeated their performance, varying it a little.

Just before dawn, when a faint light already showed in the east, the party broke up. In the darkness I could hear the splash of paddles, and men calling to each other as they returned to their houses. Each night as I lay down to sleep a cloud of mosquitoes settled on my face, and a weight of fleas moved under my blankets, but I accepted this as a small price for the contentment I had found.

My medicine box, too, helped me to win acceptance. I had never had any medical training, but by visiting hospitals and dispensaries in the Sudan and Abyssinia, and by talking to doctors, I had picked up some knowledge, and from living among tribesmen who had never seen a doctor I had acquired some experience. I treated a number of Fartus and gradually my reputation spread. Sometimes I dealt with as many as a hundred patients a day, for dysentery, for a form of non-venereal syphilis called *bajal*, for worms, sore eyes, colds, pneumonia, malaria, influenza, wounds, ulcers and many other complaints. The young men, too, no longer trusting their own practitioners, came to me to be circumcised. But there was much that I could not attempt and I had many failures. I am still haunted by the face of a small boy, dying of dysentery despite all my efforts. Often, too, it was difficult to convince them that I could do nothing. Confident that I could cure them, they would bring me, perhaps from a long distance, an old man dying in agony of cancer, or a girl coughing up her lungs with tuberculosis, and would go on begging pathetically, 'Just give us some medicine, friend; just give us some medicine'.

cf. p. 187

Living as one of them, I could take few if any precautions. Bilharzia was endemic so I avoided stepping into the water near the villages during the summer when the minute worms that cause the disease are active. I have never during my travels bothered to boil or sterilise the water I drank. Here, in any case, it would have been impracticable, but I sometimes thought ruefully that the water with which the women filled the jars must contain an interesting and varied collection of germs. During the eight years I was in the Marshes I never suffered from anything worse than a headache or a mild attack of diarrhoea.

I visited many villages; some, like Saigal near the mainland, comprised several hundred houses, others half a dozen. I treated their sick, watched the men spearing fish, and shot duck for food. Then I went back to Falih bin Majid's *mudhif*. 'Welcome. You have come back at last. You are indeed welcome. Now, by God, you are going to stay with me for a while.' I was delighted to do so.

Later in that spring of 1951 I went back to Kurdistan; but returned to the Marshes in the autumn. It was then, on a visit to Qabab, that I bought my own canoe and enlisted two Feraigat canoe-boys. One of them was Yasin: about sixteen, tall and gracefully built with the body of an athlete, he had an attractive open face. Hasan, the same age, but shorter and stockier, was a keen wildfowler and owned a fearsome muzzle-loader of local make, the barrel inadequately bound with copper wire. I persuaded him to leave this gun behind, telling him to use mine. Of the two Yasin was the dominant character and the better waterman. Although only a boy he was deemed exceptionally skilful, even by Madan standards.

cf. p. 191

Six weeks later we returned to Falih's village. I proudly showed him my canoe. He turned and gave an order to one of his servants, who went off, and came back punting a brand new *tarada*. Thirty-six feet long, dark and glistening, slim and high-prowed, she glided towards me through the water. 'She is yours, I had her specially built for you. You may like to think you are one of the Madan but in fact you are a sheikh. This *tarada* is worthy of you.' Much moved, I tried to express my thanks but Falih put his hand on my shoulder and said, 'You are my friend'.

cf. p. 202

cf. pp. 206–7

Falih suggested that I needed two other lads to complete my crew, and recommended Amara and Sabaiti. Slightly built and remarkably handsome, Amara was deft and self-possessed, a natural aristocrat. He had a quiet charm that was very engaging. In contrast Sabaiti was clumsy and far from handsome, but invariably good-natured. Although considerably younger than the other canoe-boys, Amara had the strongest character. Sabaiti followed him without question, and Hasan seldom demurred from his decisions. Only Yasin was sometimes resentful of Amara's leadership and apt to find himself in consequence the odd man out. Amara and Sabaiti soon learned to assist me with medicines, and Amara generally gave the injections.

cf. pp. 187, 191

Saying that I wanted companions not hired servants, I paid my canoe-boys no regular wage. I clothed them and gave them in fact more money than they could have hoped to earn. Later, when they got married, I helped them with their bride-price. It pleased me to hear them answer, when asked how much the Englishman paid them, 'We have no wages. We accompany our friend for pleasure. He is generous and takes care of us.'

The same wild boar that are found from India to Spain and North Africa abounded in the Marshes and the surrounding country, but here in Iraq they were often of immense size, almost certainly the largest in the world. They varied greatly in colour; one of the largest I ever shot had long, matted, dark brown hair. The coats of some were almost black, of others reddish, while a sounder we once saw were all so pale in colour that for a moment we wondered if they were sheep. Many, however, had only a few coarse bristles on their bare hides. The piglets, born between March and May and usually five to a litter, had soft, striped coats and were attractive little beasts. By day the pig frequently lay up on sodden nests, built on the low banks of irrigation ditches among the bulrush beds. The nests, sometimes six feet across, were great heaps made of rushes which had often been carried for yards. Sometimes the pig hid among the tangled vegetation of *qasab*, brambles, tall clumps of sedge, small willows and creepers, which grew on floating islands. When the floods were high they moved out of the marshes and lay up in the date gardens, often veritable jungles of untended palms and close-growing thorn scrub; I once saw a wolf and three cubs in one of these.

The Marshmen hated the wild boar, their only natural enemy after lion were exterminated following the influx of modern rifles in the First World War. I remember an old man saying, 'Pigs! They are the foe. They eat our crops and kill our men. God destroy them! Look at Manati: he will never be any use again. That sow has finished him.' And Manati lay in the bottom of a canoe, with blood oozing from a wound in his right buttock into which I could have put my fist. I treated too many people savaged by pig, and saw too many devastated rice and wheat fields, a family's livelihood destroyed overnight, to have any compunction about shooting pig. I have counted over sixty feeding at sunset on the edge of the reed-beds, and have driven them out of empty houses in an inhabited village where they had gone to lie up at dusk. I once shot as many as forty-seven in a day; I shot hundreds over the years, but without making any appreciable difference to their numbers. And although I killed them when the chance offered I should have hated to see them exterminated as lion had been. Their massive dark shapes, feeding on the edge of the reed-beds at evening, were for me an integral part of the marsh scene. Without the constant risk of encountering them life for me would have lost much of its excitement.

On one occasion I had already shot a dozen, almost kicking them out of bramble thickets along abandoned ditches, and shooting them as they broke across the open. A boy ran up bringing news of a pig he had found in some nearby wheat, pointing out the exact spot. The trampled hollow was obvious even from a distance but the crop was breast-high and as I approached I could not see down into the hollow till less than a yard away. Suddenly an ear flicked and I saw the pig lying in shadow with its back to me. I shot it in the neck and it never moved. 'Come on, let's get back; we have a long way to go', urged my host when I rejoined him at the canoe. As we were leaving the boy ran up again with news of another pig. 'Come and shoot it, friend. It is destroying all my crop.'

My host tried to dissuade me, but I said, 'Just this one and then I will be with you'. Again I stalked a hollow which the boy indicated, and peered over the top of the corn into the eyes of a big boar. I still remember the white glint of its tushes. Before I could aim I was flat on my back yards from where I had been, my rifle going off as I went down. Then the boar was on me again. I felt its weight on my thighs, saw its long snout and angry eyes above me, and smelt its breath on my face. It drove at my chest with its tushes. Instinctively I blocked the swipe with my rifle butt. Then the pig was gone. I sat up and looked at my rifle: there was a great gouge in the stock and one of my fingers was slashed to the bone, as if by a razor. The boar, a big one, was walking away on the edge of the cornfield. I shouted: it swung round. I aimed at its chest and fired. It dropped where it stood. Rarely can anyone have escaped so lightly after being knocked down by a boar. I had had a similar escape in the Sudan when I was knocked down by a lion.

On another occasion we were hunting pig in our *tarada*. The others were dragging it through shallow water when we saw two big boars about two hundred yards away across the mud flat. The boys turned the canoe sideways and stood behind it. Sitting in it I fired, and hit the larger boar. He spun round and came straight for us, the other close behind. I fired again and heard the bullet smack, but he never faltered. Then again, and still he came on. Now he was very close. I fired a fourth time and he dropped. I had one shot left. I worked the bolt and swung to face the other boar which would be on me in two more bounds. I fired my last shot and down he went, skidding right up to the boat. I reloaded. Neither boar moved. I could touch the nearer. The other was a foot or so out of reach. I had been too busy to be afraid, but the double charge and the seeming ineffectiveness of my shooting must have been very alarming to my companions, who were unarmed, my shotgun and pistol being beside me in the boat. I turned to find them half-crouched, their daggers in their hands. 'What would you have done if it had got into the boat?' 'We would have jumped on it and killed it with our daggers', Amara answered.

When it was summer in the Marshes clouds of mosquitoes hung round our heads, even in daytime as we glided along the silent passages between the dark towering reed-beds. At night they gorged on our naked bodies, for it was too hot to bear even the lightest covering. Then we were glad to leave the Marshes and travel for a while among the villages along the river, making new friends among the cultivators. But whether our journey had been long or short, we always came back in the end to Falih's *mudhif*. Someone would see our *tarada*, and Falih would be waiting on the bank to welcome us. Occasionally we returned late at night or in the early hours of morning, and bedded down in the *mudhif*. Old Abd ar Ridha, the coffee man, would find us when he came in at dawn and would hurry off to tell Falih his friend was there. One by one the shrouded figures of Falih's retainers would sit up, straighten headcloths and adjust clothes. Then they would come forward to greet me. 'Welcome, friend, welcome. This is a happy day. You have been away from us too long.' I was known everywhere as *Sahib*, which in Arabic means friend.

Falih's death 1953

Each year, when the heat and humidity of summer became intolerable I left the Marshes to travel in the mountains of Pakistan, Afghanistan or Morocco. In 1952, I was planning to travel in Chitral, and now it was time to leave. Amara, Sabaiti, Yasin and Hasan were with me on my last night in Falih's *mudhif*. In the evening we moved outside for coolness and sat on the grass. The 'forty days' wind' that blew throughout June was over some time past. Now not a breath of air stirred. As the sun set jackals yapped their brief, unearthly chorus beyond the falling river, the moon rose, and bats dipped and wheeled above our heads. We ate melons and grapes, and drank lime tea. Abd ar Ridha came with his pot of coffee and said to me, 'Have some more while you can. You won't get coffee like this where you are going.' And Falih said, 'Don't stay away from us too long'.

I came back early in February 1953 and the next day went shooting duck. Abbas, Falih's favourite nephew, fired at a bird in a reed-bed but wounded Falih who was on the far side. He had mixed up his cartridges, which looked the same. One single large LG pellet, fired at least seventy yards away, had hit Falih near the heart. Realising what he had done, Abbas ran off. We placed Falih in a large canoe and towed it along the bank towards his home two miles away. News of the accident spread across the countryside. Small groups of silent people hurried in our direction. As soon as they reached us they flung themselves shrieking into the water and plastered mud upon their heads and dripping clothes, the women tearing their garments and beating their breasts. 'Falih, my father, my father', they wailed, and followed behind us.

Only the day before he had welcomed me back to his house; now I was sure he was dying. To the others it would have been more understandable had I wept like them, but some deep-seated inhibition denied me this relief. I, who shared so much with them from choice, could not share in this expression of their grief.

Falih tried to speak. Ordering the men to stop I knelt beside the boat. 'Where is Abd al Wahid?' he whispered. 'He is coming.' His son, crippled among the thorns without his shoes which he had left in the *mudhif*, was a little way behind. 'Tell him . . . tell him from me, Sahib, that he is to take Abbas to his father. He is not to leave him until he is safe with his father. Whatever happens to me, he is to see that nothing happens to Abbas. That is my command. Tell him to take him there now.' He shut his eyes again. Abbas was presumably ahead of us, running desperately for home.

We arrived at Falih's house and carried him in. Unwilling to intrude, I remained outside until someone told me that Falih had asked for me. I went over to where he lay. He moved his eyes, looked at me but could not speak. Later his uncle arrived and they took Falih to his father in Baghdad.

I went to Baghdad next day. I asked a policeman for Majid's house and he told me how to find it, adding as an afterthought, 'but Majid has gone to Najaf to bury his son who died yesterday'.

That was how I heard of Falih's death.

Three days later I went back to Falih's village to join in the mourning. From a distance I could hear the wailing of the women and the rhythmic beating of their breasts. Several tribal banners were set in the entrance to the *mudhif*, their long red folds and the silver ornaments on the poles brilliant against the reed wall. It was very silent inside and rather dark. I crossed the room, greeted Majid and looked for a place. There were *Sayids*, descendants of the Prophet, in green headcloths, divines from Kerbala and Najaf dressed in black or white turbans, sheikhs of tribes from as far away as Kut and Nasariya, village headmen and elders, townsmen and merchants. Mostly they sat in silence, fingering their rosaries or smoking. Half a dozen figures would rise, go over to Majid, bid him farewell and leave the hall. Others would come in, sometimes two or three at a time, sometimes twenty. Majid, grey and unshaven, his great stomach bulging in front of him, looked very tired, an old broken man filled with bitterness. 'Why did it have to be Falih? Why Falih?' he burst out. 'God, now I have no-one left.'

Hysterical wailing and a fusillade of shots announced the arrival of yet another party. Through the doorway I glimpsed a tribal banner and a crowd of people, their heads and clothes smeared with wet mud.

We were ushered in to feed in a neighbouring shelter and after everyone had eaten, the visitors inside the *mudhif* and the tribesmen outside, the tribesmen danced the *hausa*, the war dance of the tribes. From each village in turn someone improvised a chant in praise of Falih and the tribesmen took it up and roared it back, their rifles held above their heads as they stamped in a massed circle round the crimson banners. The men who held the banners, whose traditional right it was to carry them into battle, shook the poles so that the silver ornaments clashed and jangled. Still stamping in time to the singing they began to fire their rifles, a few scattered shots at first, then massed firing such as I had only heard in war. The smell of powder, sharp and intoxicating, stirred them to wilder efforts. Majid called out at last, and his servants pushed into the milling crowd shouting, 'Enough, the Sheikh says enough'. We trooped back into the *mudhif*.

Remaining years 1953–56, 1958

'Your brother Falih is dead. God have mercy on him,' said Amara, tears trickling down his face. 'To me he was indeed a father. The best of all the sheikhs. Now you must use our house as your home. My father is not rich like the sheikhs; we are poor people. But our house is your home and you will always be welcome.'

Amara's village was downstream from Falih's, on the very edge of the Marshes. Sabaiti, whose father kept a small shop, lived in the same village. As we arrived, a tall boy, his shirt round his neck, splashed towards us from the edge of the marsh where men were working waist-deep in water, clearing the ground for the rice harvest. 'That is Rashiq, my brother. Last year he helped others with their rice. This year he has his own land.' The boy washed the mud off his feet and legs, dropped into the *tarada* beside Amara, kissed him and picked up a pole.

When we stopped at Amara's house a large crowd of children had gathered, waiting to help us land. 'Hansan, run and tell father that Sahib comes as our guest. Rashiq, see that the other chicks bring everything into the house.'

Thuqub, Amara's father, came out and received me with quiet courtesy. He held himself very erect but moved slowly and rather stiffly as he showed me into his house, which was small and low-roofed, each of its arches only a few reeds thick. A worn carpet was spread on a tattered mat with two cushions. A lively middle-aged woman with a kindly face greeted me. 'Welcome, Sahib, welcome to your home. God bless you.' Behind her stood two small boys, and a girl of about fifteen who half hid her face. Amara obviously ran this household, but with becoming deference to his gentle and devout old father. He now sent Rashiq off to find a kettle, and Sabaiti to his father's shop for sugar and tea. Then, helped by his small brothers and a crowd of other children he at last cornered an old rooster and slaughtered it for the midday meal. He also produced a very stale fish, but here no-one minded if a fish smelt and I had long got over my initial qualms. His mother had baked circular discs of bread to eat with the fish. Chilaib, another brother, arrived back from the marshes. A solid silent boy, unlike the gangling mischief-loving Rashiq, he was in charge of the buffaloes, and although only twelve worked from dawn till dusk, cutting and fetching reed shoots for them to eat at night. The herd comprised a wild-eyed bull, three cows and a heifer. Amara's heart was with the buffaloes. After milking he said, as he fondled a cow, 'Look at this beauty, and in calf too. I bought her with money you gave me last year. Soon, God willing, we

cf. p. 183

will have a proper herd.' This visit was the first of many.

Two Englishmen spent some time with me in the Marshes. One was the late Gavin Maxwell, who wanted to write about them and travelled with me for seven weeks. *A Reed shaken by the Wind* was a brilliant piece of verbal photography, but at such close quarters I found him trying, inclined to be querulous and neurotic. The other was Gavin Young, who has recently written the evocative *Return to the Marshes*. He had an instinctive understanding and affection for the Madan, and I always looked forward to his brief visits to me from Basra.

cf. pp. 208–9

With the passage of time those years tend to merge in my memory. 1954, the year of the flood, stands out. But in the Marshes that year life went on much as usual, inconvenienced but not seriously affected by a disaster that overwhelmed much of Iraq and even threatened Baghdad. Outside the Marshes however, we poled our *tarada* across fields of uncut corn and between the trunks of countless palms. Whole villages had been evacuated, and abandoned dogs howled in despair from the rooftops. Only Yasin's skill saved us when we swept down the Euphrates, a turmoil of racing water. The following year was the year of the drought, when whole villages lay derelict after their inhabitants migrated to Basra or Baghdad. The Madan, however, benefited that year, sowing crops of rice on ground normally deep under water.

cf. p. 193

During the eight years I was there we crossed and re-crossed the Marshes as the whim took us. We paddled through snow-white fields of ranunculus, floating on deep water; speared fish among the trailing weeds; beat down the *qasab* to make a platform on which we cooked and ate the duck that we had shot, while halcyon kingfishers flashed among the reeds and otters whistled nearby; we ventured across great expanses of open water in dread of sudden storms, and once were nearly caught and drowned; we sweated under the sun, manhandling our *tarada*, thirty-six feet of it, along narrow ditches hardly wider than the boat; and we

cf. pp. 202, 203

visited that master craftsman, Haji Hamaid, who had built it in his boatyards on the north bank of the Euphrates. In the year of the drought we watched the Berbera, despised by the tribesmen because they used nets, hauling out great loads of golden barbel. We travelled among the famous Muntifiq tribes in their palm groves along the Euphrates, and there we slept in *mudhifs* reminiscent of

cf. pp. 198–9, 201

Gothic cathedrals.

cf. pp. 182, 187

We spent most of our time in the central Marshes, but several times we crossed the Tigris and visited the Suaid, and the Heleki or 'Cormorants', and stayed among the nomad Feraigat, a lawless people constantly at feud with the villagers. To provide fresh grazing for their great herds of buffaloes, they burnt the reeds on which the villagers relied for weaving mats. We went as far as the Persian frontier and our guide, who lived by smuggling, showed us where he had ambushed and killed two Persian *gendarmes*. In these Marshes massed battalions of wildfowl darkened the surface of the lagoons. I had seen them flighting in at sunset to feed on the harvested rice fields, reminding me of swarms of locusts. I saw the wild geese arrive in October. Grey-lag and white-fronted, they came out of the north, returning from their breeding grounds on the tundras of Siberia, and in their calling was the magic of wild places. Wedge-shaped formations followed each other, strung out across the pale sky, and as I watched I thought of the inevitable day when the last wild geese were gone and there were no more lions in Africa.

Often we remained for days among our old friends at Qabab, or with Jasim and his Fartus. I watched the Fartus dance the *hausa*, as they sang in chorus of how they had stormed the Al Essa fort to liberate one of their villages; how Falaij, the last of its defenders, had shouted his war cry and jumped off the roof among them, to die under their knives. We stayed with the Al Essa on the mainland and saw the new moon that ended the month-long fast of Ramadhan. The tribe gathered next day to pay homage to Maziad, their Sheikh, and to feast in his great guest tent. At dawn they came in across the plain, some on horseback, others on foot, each contingent under its crimson banner. When at last they were assembled they charged and counter-charged on their horses, while those on foot stamped round, firing off their rifles and chanting:

> 'We will go back to the open water,
> We will go and bring back Falaij',

cf. pp. 181, 189

and I remembered hearing how Falaij had died, from the Fartus who had killed him.

In June 1958 Amara, Sabaiti and I escaped from the humid Marshes to travel for a while among the shepherd tribes in the desert. Each encampment lent us horses to take us to the next. Amara had become an accomplished horseman, but Sabaiti was never at home in the saddle. Kindest and most considerate of my four companions, he was intelligent, level-headed and good-tempered. The others could be easily provoked but he never minded their jokes: I teased him now as he bumped along beside me but he only grinned. Here I hunted wild boar with the Bani Lam in the tamarisk scrub along the river bank, riding them down and shooting them one-handed from the saddle as I drew alongside, an unconven-

cf. p. 191

tional but effective variant of pig-sticking.

I was leaving shortly for England but planned to come back later in the year. I was worried about Amara's safety. Two years previously his first cousin Badai had in self-defence killed one of the nomad Feraigat, and had then sought refuge elsewhere. Radhawi, the dead boy's father, had refused to accept blood-money and Amara, as Badai's next of kin, was involved in the blood-feud. I had with great difficulty induced Radhawi to grant Amara a six months' truce. This he now refused to renew, even when the most influential and respected of the *Sayids* asked for it. He declared he would have a life for a life. While Amara was with me in the Marshes I felt he was reasonably safe. I had given him a .275 rifle and he was an exceptionally good shot. I had given Sabaiti, Yasin and Hasan shotguns, so with my own rifle and Mauser pistol we were a heavily-armed party. After my departure, Amara would be on his own, always on guard, he and his old father taking it in turn to watch throughout the night.

With difficulty I discovered Radhawi's whereabouts and went there, but the local sheikh was reluctant to get involved. A *Sayid* and Sheikh Majid's representative were with me. Eventually Radhawi was produced, a small scrawny man with a wisp of beard and angry restless eyes. We demanded two years' truce for Amara. 'Never, not a day,' he shouted again and again as he glared at Amara, who sat on the ground beside me, motionless and impassive. My pistol was in front of me. At last I said, 'Listen, Radhawi, and listen carefully. If you refuse to give Amara a truce I will offer a hundred dinars reward for your arrest. The police are looking for you for two murders you have committed. Everyone will be after you. Your other son helped you and he too will be arrested. You will both spend years in prison. Give me the truce, or by God I go tomorrow to the Government and offer the reward. I mean this. What is more, I vow that if you ever do kill

Amara you and your son will die, whatever it costs me. Think it over.' His kinsmen led him aside. At last they rejoined us and one of them said, 'Radhawi is a good man. He will give Amara a year's truce, but no truce for Badai.' We accepted this. As an added precaution I gave my pistol to Amara when I left for England. At the airport Amara and Sabaiti kissed me farewell and Amara said, 'Come back soon.' 'Next year, if God wills,' I replied, and joined the queue.

Three weeks later I was having tea with friends in Ireland. Someone came into the room. 'Did you hear the four o'clock news? There has been a revolution in Baghdad and the Iraqi Royal family have been murdered. The mob has burnt the British Embassy . . .'

I knew then that I should never be allowed back to Iraq, never see the Marshes again, and that another chapter in my life was closed.

Southern Iraq, October 1950: the guest tent of Maziad bin Hamdan, Sheikh of the Al Essa shepherd tribe, in the desert on the north-western fringe of the central Marshes.
cf. page 163

Southern Iraq: a cultivators' village on the Adil, a branch stream leading down from the main channel of the Tigris and dispersing into the Marshes. *cf. page 165*

RIGHT] An Al Essa retainer of Sheikh Maziad at the door of the Sheikh's marshland *mudhif*, at Saigal, on the north-west edge of the Marshes. *cf. page 175*

A sheikh's reed-built *mudhif*, or guest house, on the edge of the Iraqi Marshes. *cf. pages 163–4*

LEFT]
A typical herd-boy
of the Suaid tribe.
cf. page 174

ABOVE RIGHT]
Buffaloes:
the Madan,
or marshmen,
largely depended
for their
livelihood on
these invaluable
and almost
amphibious
animals.
cf. page 174

BELOW RIGHT]
A typical village
in the heart of
the Marshes of
Iraq. During
nearly every year
from 1951 to 1958
I spent months in
this remote
world, and came
to regard it as
home. *cf. page
165*

Madan dwellings at Qabab: these houses
would be built on thick piles of rushes,
in six feet of water. *cf. page 165*

RIGHT] One of the Fartus tribe: travel anywhere in the Marshes had to be by boat. *cf. page 168*

A Madan elder. *cf. page 168*

ABOVE LEFT] Two Feraigat girls: Amara's sister and Sabaiti's sister whom Amara later married. *cf. pages 169–70*

ABOVE RIGHT] A marshwoman of the Suaid tribe. *cf. page 174*

BELOW LEFT] A *Sayid* after circumcision: his nostrils are blocked because of the belief that certain scents will delay his healing. *cf. page 169*

BELOW RIGHT] A boy of the Suaid tribe: he was a notably skilful dancer. *cf. page 174*

OVERLEAF]

Jasim al Faris, Sheikh of the Fartus.
His ready acceptance of my presence in the Marshes
led others later to accept me too. *cf. page 168*

ABOVE] Bani Lam tribesmen, with a pig I had ridden
down on horseback and shot from the saddle,
in tamarisk scrub beside the Tigris. *cf. page 175*

LEFT] One of my canoe-boys: Yasin, of the
Shaghanba tribe. *cf. page 169*

RIGHT] Another of my canoe-boys: Amara bin Thuqub,
of the Feraigat tribe. *cf. pages 169–70*

LEFT] A war dance in the Marshes, by the Fartus. *cf. page 175*

A war dance on the mainland, by the Al Essa,
enemies of the Fartus. *cf. page 175*

LEFT]
Cutting a pole
from *qasab*,
the giant reed
(*Phragmites
communis*)
which grows
everywhere in
the Marshes.
cf. page 165

ABOVE RIGHT]
Near Majar
al Kabir:
a boat
being towed
against the
current
up one of
the branch
streams
that flow
down from
the main
channel of
the Tigris
into the
Marshes.
cf. pages 163–6

BELOW RIGHT]
Madan waiting
to spear fish,
when these
break back
under the
advancing
line of canoes.
cf. page 174

ABOVE LEFT]
Plaiting split *qasab* cane,
to make mats for the roofs
and floors of houses.
cf. page 165

BELOW LEFT]
A partly-finished
qasab mat:
one like this,
8 by 4 feet,
taking two hours
of family effort
to plait, would
sell in the 1950s
for the equivalent
of a shilling.
cf. page 165

RIGHT] A boat laden
with *qasab* mats,
which are being
taken down to
Basra to be sold.
cf. page 165

BELOW] The first stage of a larger and more permanent house, which was being built by cultivators on the edge of the Marshes: these are the great reed pillars from which the arches will be formed. *cf. page 165*

BELOW AND RIGHT] Bending the uprights into arches: one of these simple houses could be put up in a day, by nomadic marshmen on the move. *cf. page 165*

ABOVE LEFT]
The interior of a large *mudhif*:
some were up to sixty feet long,
twenty wide and eighteen high,
and looked even bigger.
The *qasab* they were made of grew
up to twenty-four heet high.
cf. pages 163–4

BELOW LEFT]
The coffee-hearth in a *mudhif*:
the pillars of this building,
made of closely-bound qasab reeds,
were nine feet round.
cf. pages 163–4

RIGHT]
The doorway of a *mudhif*
on the Euphrates:
every part of such buildings –
pillars, bindings and mats –
was made of *qasab*.
cf. page 174

ABOVE] Haji Hamaid, the most renowned boat-builder in the Marshes, putting the finishing touches to my *tarada*, or sheikh's canoe, at his boatyard at Huwair on the Euphrates. *cf. page 174*

RIGHT] This *tarada*, given me by my friend Falih bin Majid, Sheikh of the Al bu Muhammad, was carvel-built and flat-bottomed, thirty-six feet long but only three and half feet at her widest beam. *cf. page 174*

FAR RIGHT] A *tarada* would be smoothly covered outside with a coating of bitumen; which is here being rolled hot on to my boat's planks, in Haji Hamaid's yard. *cf. page 174*

OVERLEAF] Madan going home from market in the evening. *cf. pages 163–6*

My *tarada* in rough water:
sudden gales in open water were
a hazard dreaded by the marshmen.
cf. page 169

FAR LEFT] *Taradas* are punted in shallow
water, paddled in deep.
cf. pages 163–6

LEFT] A boy of the central Marshes,
poling his canoe through the shallows.
cf. pages 163–6

1954, the year of
the great floods:
a gale, and
floodwater
six feet deep
covering the desert
on the western
edge of
the Marshes.
cf. page 174

OVERLEAF]
Sunset in
the Marshes.
cf. pages 163–6

Amara bin Thuqub,
my constant companion in
the Marshes from 1952–58
cf. pages 169–77

Afghanistan and Pakistan, and parts of adjacent countries

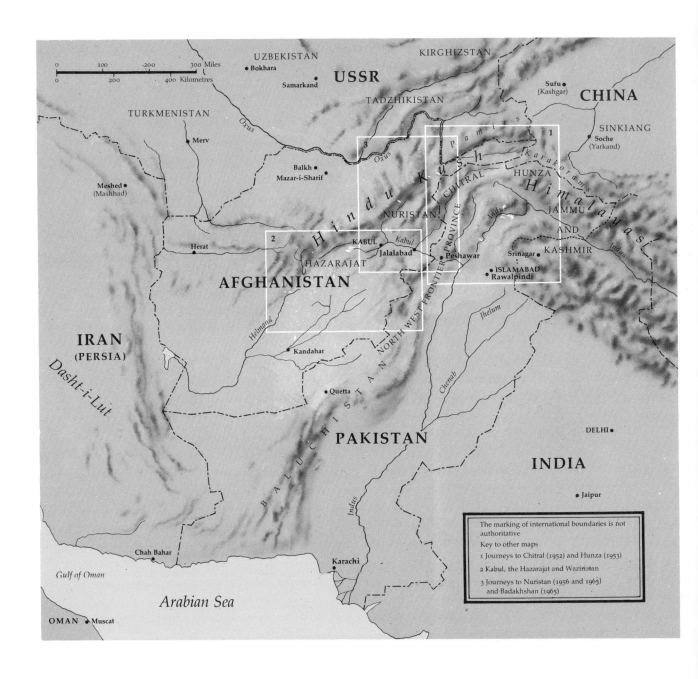

MOUNTAINS

Journeys to Chitral (1952) and Hunza (1953) *(see also key map on p. 214)*

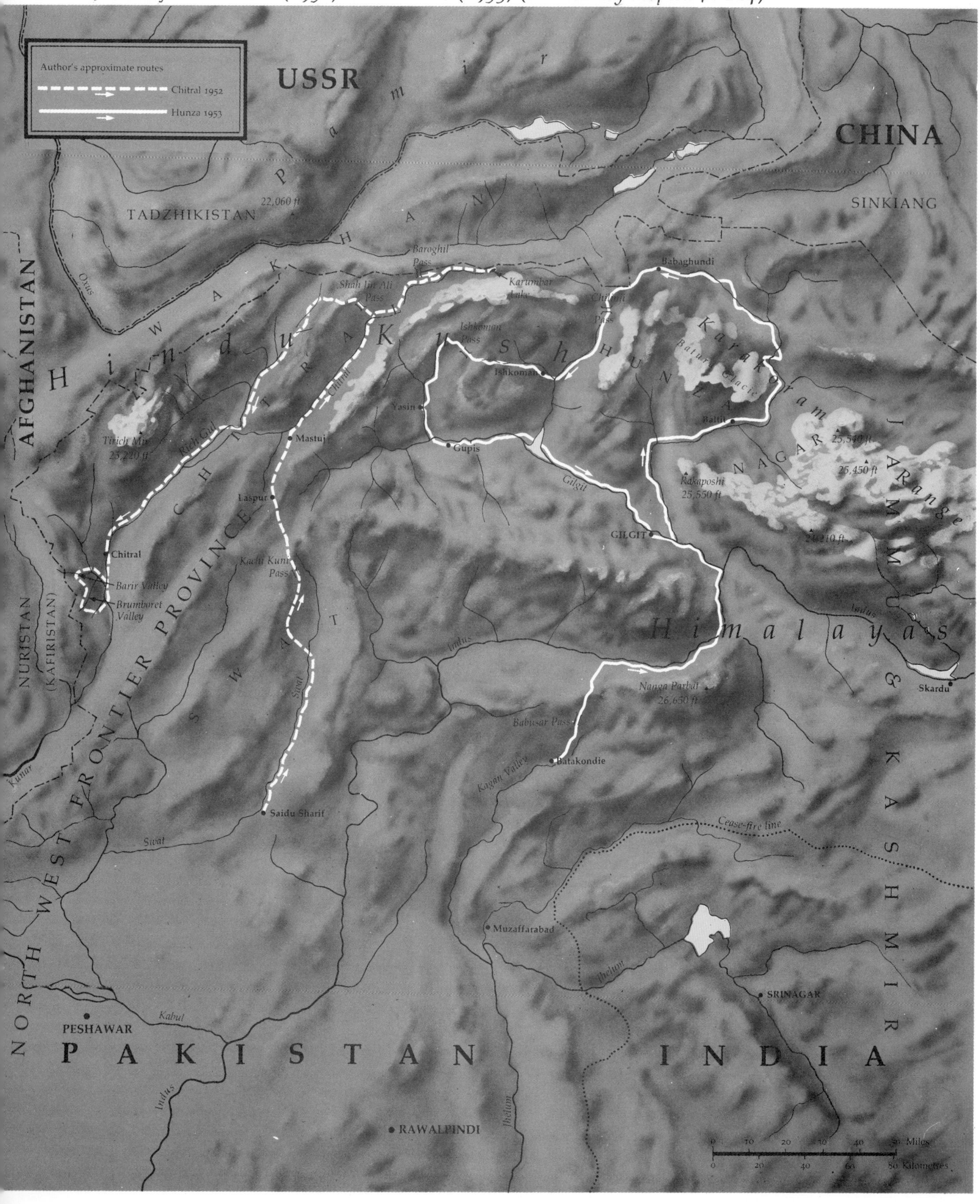

Author's approximate routes

- - - - ► Chitral 1952
———— ► Hunza 1953

USSR

CHINA

TADZHIKISTAN

SINKIANG

22,060 ft

AFGHANISTAN

Baroghil Pass

Shah Jin Ali Pass

Karambar Lake

Babaghundi

Ishkoman Pass

Karakoram

Batura Glacier

HUNZA

NAGAR

25,550 ft

25,450 ft

Tirich Mir 25,210 ft

Rich Gol

Mastuj

Yasin

Ishkoman

Baltit

Gupis

Rakaposhi 25,550 ft

J A R a n g e

Chitral

Laspur

Gilgit

25,210 ft

Kachi Kuni Pass

GILGIT

Barir Valley

Brumbwret Valley

NURISTAN (KAFIRISTAN)

H i m a l a y a s

S W A T

Indus

Nanga Parbat 26,650 ft

Skardu

NORTH WEST FRONTIER PROVINCE

Babusar Pass

Batakondie

Cease-fire line

K A S H M I R

Saidu Sharif

Kagan Valley

Swat

Muzaffarabad

Jhelum

SRINAGAR

Kabul

PESHAWAR

P A K I S T A N

I N D I A

Indus

RAWALPINDI

Jhelum

0   10   20   30   40   50 Miles

0   20   40   60   80 Kilometres

Mountains

Chitral 1952

In Abyssinia in 1944 I read *Upon That Mountain*. I had never done any climbing, indeed only once in my life have I been on a rope, but I had always hoped to travel in the Himalayas, the Karakorams or the Hindu Kush. Reading that book I was captivated by the personality of Eric Shipton and felt sympathy with his concept of mountaineering. Though a magnificent mountaineer Shipton appeared to be more essentially an explorer, more anxious to see what lay behind a mountain than to climb a still unconquered face. In 1952 he had lunch with me and advised me to travel in Hunza in northern Pakistan. I remember him saying that the view of Rakaposhi from Baltit was one of the finest he had seen.

I went to Pakistan from the Marshes in July 1952, and in Rawalpindi visited the necessary official to ask permission to travel through Chitral and back through Hunza. The curse of travelling today is the need to get permits from bureaucrats. This one was evasive, asked for my address, and said I should hear in due course. He obviously had no intention of giving me the permit. Fortunately I had a letter of introduction from Sir George Cunningham, a former Governor, to the then Governor of the North West Frontier Province. I went to Peshawar, called on the Governor, gave him the letter and came out of his house with permission to travel where I would in the states of Swat and Chitral. He was very sorry he could not give me permission to travel in Hunza, which was outside his Province.

I engaged a Pathan bearer called Jahangir Khan, who spoke some English, and went to Saidu Sharif, the capital of Swat, where I called upon the Wali, or ruler. He authorised me to cross the Kachi Kuni into Chitral, but warned me that the pass was difficult, adding that as far as he knew no European had ever crossed it. I was sure this was not so, but when I looked on those mountains I was scared. I had never seen anything like them, and I felt inadequately equipped. I had a small tent which would just take me and my bearer, a sleeping bag, a rucksack, some solid fuel and an ice-axe. That was all, except for a few personal possessions such as maps, books, a camera, a few medicines and a change of clothes. However, I have always believed that I could go wherever the locals went, travelling as they did. I knew that the people of Swat sometimes crossed this pass, and that when they did they certainly did not use ropes or other mountaineering gear. Indeed, as I was soon to discover, they set off with a cloak over a shirt and trousers, and a Chitrali cap, their bare feet just wrapped in goatskins held in place with puttees; they did not even take blankets. I would never have survived without my sleeping bag. In Saidu Sharif I bought some flour, rice, butter, dried fruit, sugar and tea, and on 26th August Jahangir Khan and I set off up the valley with two mules provided by the Wali, and an escort armed with an antiquated hammer-gun. Torrential rain had fallen the previous day and the mountain-tops were hidden in cloud. The valley was narrow and its steep sides were covered with deodars and oaks. At first we passed a succession of small homesteads, with walnut and fruit trees, and maize growing on diminutive terraces, also an occasional square fort on a spur. After three days we changed the mules for four porters. I had felt confined by the trees and the narrow valley, and was glad when we climbed higher, where deodar and oak gave place to birch.

On 31st August we slept at about thirteen thousand feet. The going had been rough and often very steep, over miniature glaciers and accumulated detritus from the cliffs above. I had pitched the little Everest tent on a small ledge, and after a meal Jahangir and I crawled into it while the porters found shelter among the rocks. It snowed heavily during the night and I was afraid the porters would refuse to go on, for it was very cold and blowing hard. However next morning without preparing any food they shouldered their loads and set off without a murmur. I went ahead, hacking steps up faces of frozen snow; never having used an ice-axe before I wasted a lot of energy, but the altitude, even when we crossed the pass at sixteen thousand feet, had little effect on me. On the far side of the pass was a large glacier covered with snow. One of the porters led the way, saying he cf. pp. 234–5 knew how to avoid the crevasses. Two days later, at the small village of Laspur, Jahangir and I hired two donkeys to carry our kit to Mastuj, another village of scattered houses, with a rest house.

I spent two days at Mastuj, where I met Colonel Khushwaqt-al-Mulk and his brother, Major Mohiuddin, relatives of the ruler of Chitral. They had arranged a game of polo and invited me to play. I had never played before but they insisted that it was time I learnt. A pipe band had played the previous night to announce the match, and it now played throughout the game. The ground had a stone wall on either side, a shallow ditch across the middle and rocks to mark the goals. We played five a side and the two chukkers were of indeterminate length. I do not suppose I hit the ball a dozen times but it was great fun. It was in these parts, and in such games as this, that polo originated.

The Colonel instructed a man called Malung and his sixteen-year-old son to take me to Karumbar where the Chitral river rises. We bought more food in the small market, and next morning, after loading a horse and a donkey with our kit, set off early. I remember wild roses in bloom along the track. Ahead of us in a clear sky the great white peak of Tirich Mir, twenty-five thousand two hundred feet, and the tallest in the Hindu Kush, towered above other snowy mountains of twenty thousand feet and more.

Each evening we stopped at some homestead. Undistinguished from the out-side, the flat-roofed houses, each surrounded by a walled orchard, were carefully constructed with massive, well-cut pillars and beams, and a funnel-shaped outlet over the hearth to let out the smoke. Hereabouts men and boys wore circular caps with wide tubular rims, and overcoats of oatmeal-coloured homespun. Many of them carried two-stringed bows that shot stones from a small leather pouch, cf. p. 237 like a catapult.

Several times during the following days we had to cross the river, sometimes on wooden cantilever bridges, but more often wading thigh-deep in the icy water, carrying the loads ourselves. Wherever the river flowed through a gorge we had to lead the animals along a crumbling track, usually high up round the shoulders of a mountain.

Except for clumps of dwarf juniper and a few willows beside the river, the landscape was bare of trees until higher up we came to scattered groves of birch already turning golden. Above the tumbling river, cliffs and screes rose to glaciers and snows glimpsed through swathes of lowering cloud or sharp and white against a blue sky. Not infrequently the mountain faces were too steep for snow to lie, and the rocks showed black, purple, brick-red, pink or ivory. On either side of the valley the ranges were cleft by gorges down which misty blue water from the snows surged among the boulders, each torrent in turn an obstacle to our animals.

cf. p. 237
Now, for the first time, I met Kirghiz, with Mongolian features and wisps of beards; Kazak and Wakih, who were refugees from Afghanistan; and people from beyond Kashgar. Their herds of yaks, long-haired, stocky beasts, most of them black but a few white or piebald, grazed on the mountain slopes above the houses.

Seven days after leaving Mastuj we reached the headwaters of the Chitral river. I left the others in the house where we had slept and, accompanied by our host, both of us on horses, set off in the bitter cold of sunrise to see the lake. In this tremendous country of great heights, under the clear blue sky of Central Asia, I had the same sense of space and cleanness that I had known in the deserts of Arabia. We rode slowly along a wide valley, past russet-coloured bogs, patched with the dark green of bog-myrtle and laced with a network of ice-fringed rivulets. Four hours later we came to Karumbar. All around us mountains, mantled with snow, sloped to a lake some three miles long, its waters a deep vivid blue. That morning we saw a surprising number of birds: several coveys of partridges, a few ravens and kestrels, an occasional hoopoe and many of the ubiquitous choughs. There were also many marmots that sat above their burrows and whistled at us as we passed.

Near the lake was a shelter like a sheep-pen; three men were sitting in it as we arrived. Two horses grazed nearby, one with a splendid Kirghiz saddle decorated with silver. I dismounted and went over to the men, who were drinking tea from small handle-less cups. One looked Mongolian and wore a mulberry-coloured surcoat, a fur-lined cap with ear-flaps, and high boots; another looked like a bearded Afghan Mullah, and the third was a Chitrali boy. I said in English, 'Good afternoon, gentlemen'. It seemed silly to say *'Salam alaikum'*, and not be able to follow it up in Persian, Turki or whatever they spoke. The Mongol smiled and answered in perfect English, 'Won't you join us?' While I was drinking tea he asked me if I spoke German. I said, 'Only French and Arabic, I am afraid', and he replied, 'My friend the Mullah speaks Arabic'. Shades of *Kim* and the 'Great Game', I thought. I felt it would be indiscreet to ask questions, but gathered that they were on their way to Kashgar where Shipton had been Consul after the Second World War. I would have given much to have travelled with them, but times had changed and the boundaries of our world had closed in.

cf. p. 236
Next day, from the Baroghil pass, I gazed out over the mountains of Wakhan and saw, far off, a glint of water which I hoped was the Oxus. There on the top of the pass it was very still; only the shadow of an occasional cloud drifted across the vast land. Then we went back down the valley on our way to the town of Chitral. We made a detour and crossed the fourteen-thousand-foot pass of Shah jin Ali into the Rich Gul valley, for I was anxious to get close to Tirich Mir. Our hosts from the night before helped us carry the loads up the pass: fully laden, our animals would never have reached the top. We followed the Rich Gul to the glaciers at the foot of Tirich Mir, crossed yet another pass at thirteen thousand feet to regain the main valley and then, travelling through fertile country where we were always hospitably entertained, arrived at Chitral.

By now I was leg-weary; during the last few days even a five-hundred-foot climb had been an effort. It was no wonder: I had covered some three hundred and fifty miles of mountainous country since leaving Saidu Sharif in Swat a month before.

After a few days' rest I visited the Black Kafirs' villages in the valleys of Brumboret and Barir to the south of Chitral. People there still worshipped the old gods, grew grapes for wine, and set up carved wooden figures where they buried their dead. Their kinsmen across the border had been forcibly converted to Islam by Abd er Rahman, Amir of Afghanistan at the end of the last century, and their land, once known as Kafiristan, was now called Nuristan, 'Land of Light'. I was later to travel through Nuristan but I am glad I saw the people here as they once had been throughout Kafiristan.

Back in Peshawar I found a letter from the bureaucrat in Rawalpindi, much regretting that it was impossible to consider my application for permission to travel either in Chitral or Hunza.

Hunza 1953

The following year I again spent the hot weather in Pakistan, reaching Karachi on 6th August 1953. Since independence Karachi had become a boom city, much of it a jumble of half-built concrete buildings or of squalid shacks. It was an unattractive place, particularly at that season of hot and humid weather when torrential storms were apt to flood the streets.

Martin and Monica Moynihan, from the British High Commission, very kindly had me to stay: this helped me endure a really frustrating month. The Prime Minister sanctioned my proposed journey through Gilgit and Hunza, but was then deliberately obstructed by the Minister for Kashmir Affairs, whose office issued the permits. Finally, after a row between them in Cabinet, I was given the necessary papers.

I went next day to Peshawar, engaged an English-speaking Pathan called Faiz Muhammad, and left by car for Batakondie. There I hired two mules to take us up the Kagan valley and over the Babusar pass, where we encountered large numbers of Gujur tribesmen. Some of these fine-looking nomads were camped in black tents on the hillsides; others, with their buffaloes, cattle, sheep and goats, were on the move along the track. A few of their women, dressed completely in white with lattice-work veils, rode on mules or horses; most of them, unveiled and with their hair in plaits, went on foot. From the top of the Babusar pass we had a view of Nanga Parbat, and then a descent of twelve thousand feet in twenty-five miles. The Indus valley was spectacular, far more so than the Kagan, but I was anxious to push on: my journey would not really start until I had passed beyond Gilgit.

Faiz Muhammad and I left Gilgit in mid-September with a local man and his two pack-horses. Two days later we had our first glimpse of Rakaposhi, over twenty-five thousand feet high, and twenty thousand above us. For the next three days we saw this incredible mountain, crowned with dazzling pyramids of snow and ice, rising abruptly from the far side of the great valley up which we travelled. I remembered Shipton describing Rakaposhi in the Travellers' Club, and how this had fired me with desire to see it. Now I had done so: whatever lay ahead the journey was worthwhile.

cf. p. 239

We travelled along a broad shelf of fertile land, with mountains on one side and a sheer cliff on the other, falling to the wide bed of the river. We passed farmsteads, orchards and cultivated fields. Men dressed in cloaks, similar to those worn in Chitral, thrust grapes and peaches on us as we walked past, or welcomed us into their homes for the night. We reached Baltit, where we stayed for two days as the guests of the Mir, an impressive and friendly man who spoke excellent English. Then, with two fresh pack-horses, we set off again, through the heart of the Karakorams towards the Pamirs. The country was unbelievably impressive, even more so than Chitral the year before.

We were now following the route that led eventually to Kashgar; sometimes the track ran beside the river, a racing torrent flecked a dirty grey with flakes of mica; sometimes it climbed over a shoulder to avoid a gorge. On either side of the valley jagged, serried peaks rose for thousands of feet, dwarfing into insignificance whole villages on the floor below; and yet these peaks were only the pleated skirts of mountains that lay behind, snow-covered and immense. The hamlets became fewer and more scattered, the mountainsides were now bare rock and scree, devoid of vegetation. We reached the Batura glacier, a tumbled mass of boulders, stones and earth, the underlying ice visible only in a few crevasses. It looked impracticable for our ponies, but we picked a way across with difficulty. Above us were sheer cliffs of many colours: pale orange, rusty red, umber, dun, slate grey.

Four days later we changed our horses for two yaks and four porters. We loaded the yaks; the porters would take over when we reached the formidable Chilinji pass, some seventeen thousand feet high. The yaks moved maddeningly slowly, making perhaps two miles an hour. Every now and then one or other, feeling skittish, would prance about with its tail in the air: never in my life have I seen anything so ridiculous.

We reached the shrine at Babaghundi. A small building with a wooden roof, surrounded by a low wall, it was decorated with many flags, mostly white; a great number of ibex horns, some very large, were piled in a monumental heap outside. We crowded into an empty building nearby, for it was bitterly cold and the weather looked lowering and unsettled. Just before sunset three Kirghiz turned up on yaks. They wore dark clothes, thickly padded, and black fur caps. Drab, uncouth figures on strange beasts, they had come down from the passes of the north and to me they brought the lure of Inner Asia, and forbidden lands.

cf. p. 238

Two days later, on 29th September, we camped at the foot of the Chilinji pass. Next morning we started at 5.15, but a cliff soon forced us to abandon the yaks. In this arctic landscape there seemed nothing for them to eat, but the porters assured me that the yaks would scratch about and find enough beneath the snow, and be all right until they came back for them. Beyond the cliff the going was reasonably easy, much of it up a glacier. I was worried about crevasses but the porters appeared unconcerned; they trudged steadily ahead, seldom stopping to rest. We reached the top at one o'clock and rested there a while, looking over range upon range of mountains, all of which Tilman, who had crossed this pass some years before, had described as 'looking eminently unclimbable'. But we had to get down into the valley before night fell. Immediately beneath us was a very steep slope. At first glance it looked impassable, but luckily the snow was soft and we slipped and slithered down for two thousand feet, falling frequently. Had the snow been frozen I do not think we should have ever got down.

cf. p. 241

We camped at 4.30 among some willows where we made a big fire, fed and then slept on the bare rocks round the fire. On the evening of the following day we sheltered under an overhanging rock. All that night it snowed and all the next day too. We struggled downhill for an hour that morning until we found a larger cave, and there we lay up, half-stifled by smoke from the fire that we kept burning. It dawned clear and the day remained sunny, but three feet of snow had fallen and the going was laborious. For a mile or so we followed the tracks of a snow leopard that appeared to have chosen the easiest route; eventually we came to thickets of juniper, willow and birch, among which grew some wild roses. Above us on the cliffs we saw ibex; we were to see many others further on.

Some days later we crossed the snout of the Karumbar glacier, and on 6th October reached Ishkoman, one of four small states in that area. From here two of the four Hunza porters went back to their village, but Mirza, the eldest of them, and Latif, the youngest, remained with me. All of them were splendid people, cheerful and indefatigable, and I regretted that I could not communicate with them except through Faiz Muhammad.

I was now anxious to cross the Ishkoman pass to get to Gupis, another of these small states. The pass was only fourteen thousand feet high, but the Rajah warned me that after the recent snow we might find it impassable. I therefore decided to engage four new porters, making six in all. We spent a day at Ishkoman, entertained by the Rajah, and next day, after seven hours' march, found three empty houses, used only in the summer, in one of which we slept. We kept a fire burning all night but even so by morning water in a mug was frozen solid.

We set off early but after only two and a half hours' march the Ishkoman porters wanted to camp among a few scattered birches, saying it was a long way to the pass. Since the pass appeared to me to be only a couple of hours away I determined to press on, for the weather looked unsettled and if it snowed again we would never get over. This turned out to be a serious mistake. We soon came to a flat plain about three miles wide, where the snow was deep. It took us four hours to cross, breaking through the crust at every step. After this came a succession of steep ascents and snow-filled hollows. We toiled forward foot by foot and every time I thought that we had reached the top there was yet another basin to trudge round or across, yet another ridge to climb. Finally we reached the pass at 5.30, half an hour before the sun would set. I knew there would be no moon that night. Right across the topmost ridge we found the fresh tracks of a large bear. That stimulated my porters, who were very weary, and even spurred on Faiz Muhammad, who was by now in tears, though carrying nothing. Below the pass I could see a long, steep glacier, deep in snow, and an even steeper snow-covered mountainside.

I realised we should have to keep off the glacier for fear of crevasses, and went ahead, followed by Mirza, to break a trail for the others. The Ishkoman porters, rather a poor lot, and my now hysterical bearer, were strung out behind, shepherded by Latif. It was a brute of a descent; in places I sank to my armpits through the frozen crust, but even so Mirza and I went too fast and after about two thousand feet we had lost contact with the others. By then it was dark. We shouted and shouted, but got no answer. Mirza urged me to go down to tree-level, but I was determined to wait; anyway, we had no matches. Eventually Mirza slipped away and I was left by myself on the mountainside in the freezing cold. I went on shouting at intervals and two hours later the four Ishkoman porters loomed up.

I was thankful to see them, for by then I was afraid that I would have to spend the night there and would probably lose fingers and toes. They made me understand that Faiz Muhammad had collapsed by a rock overhang, and that Latif had stayed with him. As Latif was carrying a roll of bedding I was not unduly worried about them. We continued down the mountainside, the porters going very slowly, which meant long cold waits for me. The last five hundred feet were extremely steep. At the bottom of this precipice we found some scrub and lit a fire. The porter carrying the tent had apparently stayed beneath a rock above the last descent. I got into my sleeping bag and spent a cold, wet night, for the warmth of my body melted the snow beneath. By now it was 12.30; we had been on the move for nineteen hours. Lying awake, I knew that I had made a mess of things by ignoring local advice.

The missing Ishkoman porter showed up at first light, and after a quick mug of tea I climbed back alone up the mountain to look for Faiz Muhammad and Latif. I was tired, my pack was heavy, and the ascent was steep and difficult. I was relieved when I met them, two and a half hours later. Latif was cheerful, Faiz Muhammad doleful; his feet were slightly frost-bitten. Mirza, who had gone on cf. p. 240 down to a village the previous night, had come back with several men to help us.

We now had an easy journey to Gilgit, arriving there on 18th October 1953, forty days after Faiz Muhammad and I had set off on foot up the Kagan valley. I had finished my second journey in Pakistan, and my thoughts for the coming year turned to Afghanistan, and to Nuristan in particular. Here would be scope for travel in a region that was very little known.

Those two journeys among the mountains of the Hindu Kush and Karakorams had been for me a tremendous experience, both visual and physical. I had seen the land as I wished to see it, accompanied by people who lived in it, and I had travelled through it as they did. I had been frustrated, it is true, by inability to communicate with them. This had deprived me of the sense of comradeship so important to me in Arabia and the Marshes. But I was thankful that I had not gone there with members of my own race, as one of a large, meticulously organised expedition. I should have hated, in those surroundings, to listen to the wireless, the news, sports commentaries and European music; it would have seemed utterly incongruous. All I ever want to bring with me from our civilisation are some books, and those I had, though there had been little opportunity to read them. In Arabia I had learnt to move from one world to another as easily as changing clothes, but I always tried to keep the worlds apart.

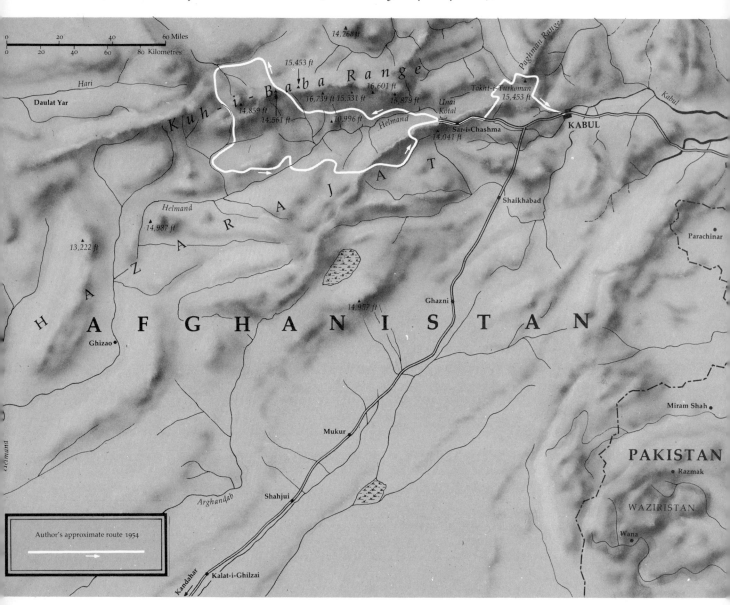

The Hazarajat 1954

I had already seen the mountains of Nuristan from the villages of the Black Kafirs in Chitral, and resolved to go there. I found, however, that permission to enter that virtually unadministered region would be difficult to obtain. Therefore when I arrived in Kabul in 1954, I asked instead for permission to travel in the Hazarajat. This, I knew, would be more easily forthcoming. By first travelling there I hoped to establish my reputation in the eyes of the Afghan Government, so that another year they would give me a permit for Nuristan. The Hazarajat was in any case a most interesting area.

I left Kabul on 10th August with the necessary permit and with Jan Baz, an interpreter provided by the government. I was fortunate to have him with me; although a townsman he endured the inevitable hardships without complaint, and during a journey of nearly four hundred miles showed patience and tact in handling the Hazaras.

At Unai Kotal, a pass over the Paghman range, we hired a man with a pony on which to carry our kit. The three pools of Sar-i-Chashma where the Kabul river rises were nearby, and we visited them, a startling experience. As we approached the first pool a dark and seemingly solid wave of fish heaved up at us, some of them lifted almost out of the water. Protected by ancient custom, these fish, a species of barbel, were fed by visitors with handfuls of maize. We were told that they disappeared for three months in the spring.

Jan Baz and I now travelled for six weeks in the Hazarajat, visiting three of its four districts, crossing and re-crossing the Kuh-i-Baba range, fording and re-fording the Helmand river, before travelling through more difficult country to the great peak of Takht-i-Turkoman, in the Paghman range; and thence back to Kabul.

I had been able to find out little about the Hazaras more recent than the thirteen pages devoted to them in the *Gazetteer of Afghanistan* published in 1882. Genghis Khan's son Jagatai, or his grandson Mangu, may have settled the Mongol ancestors of the Hazaras to guard the marches here. If so it is unlikely that they would all have belonged to one tribe; more probably they were followers of chiefs selected for their loyalty from different tribes and races in the Mongol army. During this journey I was struck by the wide range of types who called themselves Hazaras. The Hazaras number about a million, belong to the Shia sect of Islam,

cf. pp. 242, 243

and now speak a dialect of Persian.

The Kuh-i-Baba forms the spine of the Hazarajat. This high mountain range, upwards of fifteen and sixteen thousand feet, runs from east to west for about eighty miles and forms the western extremity of the Hindu Kush. It is separated from the wilder and more forbidding Paghman range by the Helmand river that rises on the northern slopes of those mountains. The Kuh-i-Baba is an uninspiring range of generally uniform height, with few peaks, none of any size, and only a few cliffs. Both sides of the mountain are seamed with a succession of valleys, and the sides of the valleys, although usually steep, consist mostly of earth or scree covered with thistles, coarse grass, hogweed, wild rhubarb and cushion-plants.

I had supposed that the Hazarajat was a desperately poor country. My first view, as I looked out across a succession of deep valleys and over bare, stony, rolling hillsides parched and tawny-coloured, certainly confirmed this impression. In the valley below I could see only a few patches of cultivation, green and conspicuous in this empty landscape. But I soon realised that this first impression was false, and due to the configuration of the land. In fact, almost every fold and wrinkle of mountainside to which water could be channelled was cultivated. As we walked up any valley it seemed that round the next corner the cultivation would inevitably peter out; and yet it went on, sometimes widening and sometimes narrowing, until eventually we came to the high valleys where all cultivation ceased. The ploughing was done with oxen, and it was surprising on what steep slopes they were used.

Although the Hazaras were primarily agriculturalists they owned large flocks of sheep and goats and some small black humped cattle. These people seldom ate meat except during certain days of Muharram, which commemorates the martyrdom of the Prophet's grandson, Hussein. Then tens of thousands of sheep and goats were slaughtered, and their meat was eaten at the mosques, where everyone assembled to hear the sacred readings. In summer many of the villagers moved with their flocks to camps on the high pastures, and there they lived in crude stone circles roofed with bushes over a framework of poles.

In some of the valleys the houses were strung out along the hillside above a narrow ribbon of cultivation, farmhouse succeeding farmhouse; in others they were grouped in small villages, one village often separated from the next by miles of stony track. The houses were built of mud and stone, usually with three or four rooms and a narrow passageway, and most were very primitive. The windows were small, set high up, admitting little light, even in summer. Several houses often adjoined and shared a common earthen roof; sometimes one roof covered an entire village. Owing to the scarcity of timber the rooms were usually small, and roofed with a dome built of stones. These domes rose above the flat expanse of roof among cut thistles, rhubarb leaves, stacks of straw, and other fodder; and heaps of artemisia and cushion-plants collected with piles of dry dung for fuel. In most villages there were watch-towers, either in the village itself or on the surrounding hills to guard the approaches. The chiefs usually lived in large well-constructed rectangular forts built round a court. Towers guarded the corners of a fort, and the single entrance could be closed with a strong wooden door. Nowhere did we encounter any towns or even large villages.

During the winter months the cold in these mountain villages is intense. Snow usually starts to fall in November, and soon makes travel outside the villages almost impossible for the next six months. Some of the Hazaras used crude snow-shoes. I was constantly surprised that such large communities could survive throughout the winter under these conditions at altitudes of eight to twelve thousand feet. Not only were there no trees here, except a few poplars grown for poles, but no scrub or bushes. Dried dung and various plants such as artemisia were an adequate if unsatisfactory fuel for cooking, but would hardly warm a house unless burnt in quantities impossible to obtain.

Already, at the end of August, it was freezing hard at night on the northern slopes of Kuh-i-Baba, and the cows, sheep and goats were brought into the houses. Four or five cows and some sixty sheep and goats would thrust in through the narrow doorway and disappear down a dark passage into the bowels of the house. During the summer and autumn any of the men or boys who could be spared from the fields set off up the mountain soon after sunrise, and spent the day carrying down great loads of hogweed and other plants, which during the winter they broke up and fed to the animals. I saw only a dozen horses during my journey, though the *Gazetteer of Afghanistan* had estimated the Hazara cavalry in tens of thousands.

There was much about the Hazaras that I admired. Most of them had attractive and some of them beautiful faces. Excellent farmers making every possible use of their uncompromising land, and skilled shepherds, they were a tough, hard-working people. Here no-one pilfered. We slept on their roofs with perfect confidence that our possessions would never be stolen. We avoided their rooms, unless the cold was intense, because of the bugs; one morning I killed sixty-two that I found in my sleeping bag. The Hazaras, however, were almost always inhospitable to our unimpressive party. When we prepared to halt in a village someone would invariably come forward and suggest that we should find better quarters in the next village. They were never unfriendly; just inhospitable.

Large numbers of nomad Pathans from the Ahmadzai, Safi and Mohmand tribes travelled up the valleys in the early summer, to their grazing grounds on the mountain-tops where they lived in black tents, until in the autumn they returned down the valleys, on their way to winter in Pakistan. These nomad Pathans were known by various names: in Pakistan as *Powindah*, generally in Afghanistan as *Kuchis*, but to the Hazaras as *Afghans*, and in the far north as *Kandaris*. They possessed large numbers of camels and great flocks of sheep and goats. The Hazaras detested them, a constant reminder that in 1892 the Afghan Amir Abd er Rahman had subdued their country. The Pathans for their part despised the Hazaras – it was the age-old conflict between nomad and farmer, the Desert and the Sown. The fact that the Pathans were Sunni, the Hazaras Shia, added a religious element to this mutual antipathy.

I had always longed to visit the North West Frontier and see the Pathan tribes – Mahsuds, Wazirs, Afridis, Mohmands and others. I had stayed for a while in 1952 with the Pakistani Political Officers at Wana and Miram Shah. I had then seen places with names made famous by the border fighting that had flickered and flared along this frontier. I had visited Razmak, once the bastion of British military ascendancy in the tribal territory; its site was marked by coils of rusting wire, and ugly barrack buildings with broken window panes, a sorry contrast with the splendid forts left elsewhere by the Moguls. But in those parts I had to travel in a car with an armed escort, necessary no doubt but irksome, and I had watched enviously as the Powindah, or Kuchis, brought their long trains of laden camels, ponderous beasts, dark and shaggy-haired, shuffling down through the passes out of Afghanistan, each man carrying a rifle over his shoulder and marching *cf. pp. 244, 245* with an unconscious swagger.

Now, two years later, I was travelling on foot among them. Here on the slopes of Kuh-i-Baba they came out of their tents as we led our pony past, pressed us to drink tea with them, to share a meal, or spend the night: the Hazaras did none of these things. The Kuchis were colourful, the Hazaras drab; the Kuchis danced and sang to drum and flute, the Hazaras never did. Despite this, I still found the Hazaras alluring, even at the end of a six weeks' journey among them. The journey had been uneventful, the country dull, but the redeeming feature had been the people, Kuchis and Hazaras alike.

USSR

Oxus

Jazira-i-Ortatugha

Oxus

Kokcha

B A D A K H S H A N

Shiva

Lake Shiva

15,602 ft

Author's approximate routes

— Nuristan (1956 and 19...)
— Badakhshan (1965)

PASHAIE Tribal names

USSR

▲ 20,000 ft

TADZHIKISTAN

Faizabad

Baharak

P a m i r

Jurm

17,569 ft

WAKHAN

Journeys to Nuristan (1956 and 1965)
and Badakhshan (1965)

(*see also key map on p. 214*)

Sar-i-Sang

Kokcha

19,198 ft

16,029 ft

20,448 ft

H i n d u K u s h

17,070 ft

Tirich Mir
25,220 ft

Anjuman

Shahr-i-Munjan

Barir
Valley

Chitral

Chitral

A F G H A N I S T A N

21,112 ft

Brumboret
Valley

Mumm Pass
18,832 ft

Utng-i-Matral

Bashgul

Chamar Pass

N U R I S T A N

1965

Mir Samir
19,880 ft

Puchal

Kamdesh

Purdm Pass 16,908 ft

1956

1956

Kantiwar Mum

15,651 ft

H

1956 and 1965

Panjshir

1956

Ramgul

Kulam

1965

Parun

Waigul

Kamu

Waigul

1965

P R O P E R

Pech

17,100 ft

(K A F I R I S T A N)

1956

Minjival

1965

1965

Kunar

N O R T H W E S T F R O N T I E R P R O V I N C E

P A K I S T A N

Panjshir

1956 and 1965

L A G H M A N   K O N A R H A

PASHAIE

Alingar

Kabul

KABUL

Kabul

Kunar

Swat

Kabul

JALALABAD

Kabul

Kabul-Jalalabad-Peshawar road

Khyber Pass

Kabul

0   10   20   30   40   50 Miles

0   20   40   60   80 Kilometres

Sefid Kuh Range
15,215 ft

PESHAWAR

Nuristan 1956, 1965   My brief visit to the Kafirs in Chitral in 1952 had made me keen to travel in Nuristan itself. After my Hazarajat journey of 1954 I was given permission in 1955, but by then had arranged to visit the High Atlas, so I eventually went to Nuristan in July 1956.

Comparatively few Europeans had travelled in Nuristan: in 1826 and 1828 Colonel Alexander Gardner, a soldier of fortune among the Afghans, twice passed through *Kafiristan*, 'Land of Unbelievers', as it was then known; in 1883 W. W. MacNair visited the Bashgul valley. This valley was more thoroughly explored in 1885 by Colonel Woodthorpe of the Indian Survey, accompanied by Sir William Lockhart. These appear to have been the only Europeans to travel in this country until Sir George Scott Robertson spent a year in the Bashgul valley in 1889–90, only seven years before the Amir Abd er Rahman overran Kafiristan, renaming it *Nuristan*, 'Land of Light', and forcibly converting its inhabitants.

I had read Robertson's *The Káfirs of the Hindu-Kush*. He admired their reckless bravery, their powers of physical endurance and their hospitality, but he deplored the pride they took in killing, whether man, woman or child. He also wrote that it was 'as natural for them to steal as to eat', and that 'their avarice was almost a mental disease'. I noticed that his map showed in some detail the configuration of all Kafiristan, large areas of which none of these travellers had visited. Gardner, escaping to Yarkand after his party had been massacred, would scarcely have mapped the area through which he passed. The work must have done by those dauntless, anonymous individuals, British and Indian, who worked for the Survey of India and at risk to their lives mapped the country across the border. It was about Kafiristan that Kipling wrote in 1888 his powerful story, *The Man who would be King*. After 1928 some eastern and southern areas of Nuristan had been visited by two German expeditions and one Danish.

The Nuristanis evidently belong to the Dardic branch of the Indo-European family. Some writers have suggested that they are descendants of Greek garrisons left behind by Alexander, when that god-like figure, sweeping like a comet across the world, passed down the Alingar valley. Others maintain that ancestors of the Nuristanis were here three thousand years ago, long before Alexander.

Now, with an Afghan to interpret, a local boy to cook and two Tajiks with horses to carry our loads, I travelled up the Panjshir valley towards the Chamar pass leading at sixteen thousand six hundred feet into Nuristan. One evening I encountered two exhausted Englishmen: desiccated, wind-chapped, lame, with bandaged hands, they looked in thoroughly bad shape. Eric Newby and Hugh Carless were returning from their valiant attempt to climb with inadequate equipment the twenty thousand foot Mir Samir, that loomed at the head of the valley. We camped together and Newby included an amusing description of our meeting in *A Short Walk in the Hindu Kush*.

We got the horses over the Chamar pass and on the far side met our first Nuristanis in one of the summer camps where they herd their cattle, sheep and goats. My Tajiks were apprehensive – I had had difficulty persuading any of them to come with me to Nuristan. The men and boys bounded up hill towards us. Dressed in dark homespun coats and baggy trousers, floppy Chitrali caps, and red scarves loosely knotted round their necks, the noisy bare-foot crowd dragged us down to their stone shelters to entertain us. There were no women here. They were banned from the *ailoq* or summer camps – their task was to tend the fields, at which no man would help them. Some of the men were six feet tall; all were bearded; they were light-skinned with brown or occasionally fair hair; many had grey eyes. Erratic by nature, they raced about or flung themselves on the ground; asked innumerable questions, then suddenly lost interest. I sensed a streak of unpredictable violence in their nature, confirmed some days later when a man walking with us and arguing with one of my Tajiks suddenly hurled him to the ground, drew his dagger and would have murdered him had I not intervened. He claimed the Tajik owed him money. After some discussion the Tajik admitted the debt, so I handed the money over. The Nuristani then remained with us as our guide, as friendly and good-natured as before.

We reached Puchal, a fair-sized village of flat-roofed houses scattered on the steep hillside above the rushing Ramgul river. Many of the villagers used chairs, some backed with ibex horns. Newby and Carless had passed this way: now a few days later another Christian had arrived. It was too much for the Mullahs, who were outspokenly hostile to this intrusion by infidels into the Land of Light.

cf. p. 252

We explored some way down the Ramgul valley, then came back to Puchal and tried to get our horses over the Purdem pass to the Kulam valley, but the descent proved impossible for them. We found shelter for the night in an *ailoq,* but next morning the shepherds insisted that we must leave at once. They had had word of brigands, armed with rifles, looking for us – they said they did not care where we were killed as long as it was not in their camp. As usual on journeys in these parts I was unarmed, so we returned once more to Puchal where we met with hysterical denunciation from a Mullah. I paid off the owners of the horses and looked for porters. The villagers were not unfriendly but, glad to profit from our predicament, they asked exorbitant rates. With four porters we crossed into Kulam and went down to Laghman, passing through the country of the Pashaie. They too had been Kafirs, or unbelievers, but they differed from the other Nuristanis: darker in colour, gentler in appearance, and speaking a separate language. They painted their eyelids, and sometimes their eyebrows, and the young men and boys, often naked to the waist, wore necklaces, and flowers in their caps. From Laghman I went to Jalalabad, then on to Peshawar, and back to the Marshes of Iraq. I had spent five weeks in Nuristan.

cf. pp. 250, 252

It was nine years before I returned, in June 1965, and then I stayed till the end of September. Again I crossed the Chamar pass, this time with six Tajik porters, and an Afghan student as interpreter. The pass was deep in snow: high on the northern face it was eroded into frozen pinnacles two feet high and a foot or so apart, the formation known to mountaineers as *névés pénitents*, laborious to cross. We were to meet it again on the Munjan pass.

cf. pp. 246–7

This time even the Mullahs welcomed me in Puchal. Throughout this journey I remained on good terms with the Nuristanis. Unlike Robertson, I never had anything stolen by them, nor did I find them avaricious. They would drive a hard bargain, but many of them, especially in villages unused to Europeans, were exceedingly hospitable. My only real disagreement with them occurred in a small village where the people gave us food on our arrival; we gorged on mulberries with bread and curds. Unwilling to impose the eight of us on them again in the evening, I bought with difficulty a chicken and we fed ourselves. The villagers were furious, said we had scorned their hospitality, and refused to see us off in the morning. I liked and admired the Nuristanis, but mistrusted the Gujurs who lived in some of the valleys: a furtive, darker people, they bore no resemblance to the

230

Gujurs I had encountered near the Babusar pass on my way to Gilgit. There were no nomad Pathans in Nuristan.

Three river systems drain the mountains of Nuristan. In the west the Ramgul and the Kulam join to form the Alingar. Then the Kantiwar and the Parun become the Pech, which, joined lower down by the Waigul from the east, flows into the Kunar. In the east is the Bashgul, which enters the Kunar higher up. This Kunar is the river which rises in Karumbar to flow past Chitral. Both Alingar and Kunar enter the Kabul river, a main tributary of the Indus.

Nuristan was a land of great contrasts, reminding me sometimes of Kurdistan but on a vaster scale. From the passes we looked over successive ranges one upon the other, each crest speckled black through the white. To the north, peaks as high as Mir Samir marked the watershed between the Indus and the Oxus, between Nuristan and the lands to the north, Munjan, Badakhshan and far off Kirghizstan.

We scrambled down from those passes, sometimes into a defile so narrow that overshadowing precipices blocked out all but a strip of sky; we crossed icy torrents on snow bridges, and passed the first trees growing wherever roots could take a hold; we descended through forests of cedar and pine, juniper, holly-oak, wild walnut and olive, and came at last to the valley bottom. I remember one spot in particular, where the untroubled river idling past dragged at the overhanging willows; where black cattle, watched by boys with flutes, grazed on rich pasture among banks of lilac primulas, purple orchids, asphodel and grass of Parnassus; where bearded bare-footed men jogged past, carrying down from their camps glistening skins of butter weighing fifty pounds and more, tied to their backs in a frame of two crotched sticks. Sometimes descending a valley we were faced by a gorge where a weight of water hurled itself against the cliffs and our only way was cf. p. 255 up notched tree trunks placed against the polished rocks.

cf. pp. 251, 254 We looked upwards at villages clinging to bastions of pale-coloured rock thousands of feet high, each jutting house propped on stilts and seeming as small as a swallow's nest. We looked down on villages cramped between the river and abrupt wooded slopes, that rose by screes to precipices and snow. I remember a small village called Mum, on the massive promontory overlooking the confluence of the Kantiwar and Parun rivers. We reached it hot and exhausted after a long, stiff scramble, but cloud swirled among the cedars, intermittently shutting out the valley, and we were soon chilled; the villagers lit a fire, gave us food and were very friendly. I remember another larger village, among mulberry trees on a gently sloping hillside, dominated by a rectangular fort. We lazed in the sun among a mass of wild flowers. There was a school here for training Mullahs, and young students came and sat with us, incongruously like dancing-boys with their long cf. pp. 248–9, 252 hair and painted eyes.

We stopped in villages of two and three hundred houses, down on the level where the valleys widened out. Women toiled all day in cultivated places, strips of wheat, maize or millet; or tended little vegetable patches. All cultivation in Nuristan was irrigated. Up on the flat and often contiguous roofs, where mulberries and apricots dried in the sun, we were given grapes to eat. At night animals were stalled beneath the rooms where we slept.

One memorable village was Burg-i-Matral near Kamdesh in the Bashgul valley. Here the wooden facings on fronts and sides of houses were carved in intricately varied patterns. Robertson disparaged this woodwork: I thought it superb. Kamdesh had recently been made accessible from Kabul by road, and it was now

fashionable in the Embassies to visit Nuristan by driving as far as Kamdesh. The
results were predictable.

cf. pp. 253, 255, 256

The Nuristanis had retained their individuality as a race even after conversion
to Islam. Now they would be visited by an ever-increasing number of expeditions
seeking adventure in wild places. This would disrupt a society utterly unpre-
pared. Each expedition by its very presence would help to destroy what it had
come to find.

Waigul, in the Waigul valley, was another interesting village, of houses clinging
to the limestone cliff. Here the supporting pillars inside the houses were elabor-
ately carved, and many doors and sideposts were adorned with stylised patterns
of ibex or markhor horns. Sometimes actual markhor horns flanked the entrance,
the skulls set one above another, or they were used to decorate the outside walls.
Some of these horns were larger than any recorded by Rowland Ward. On one
house there were sixteen heads. Markhor heads were often leant against the
carved wooden coffins of the dead; these were left in the open and sometimes we
were sickened by the stench. It was as well that there were no hyaenas or they
would soon have tugged out the corpses. Frequently elaborately-carved wooden
ornaments had been set up near the coffins, but owing to the influence of Islam

cf. p. 257

none of them now represented human figures.

I was keen to visit Shiva lake in Badakhshan, where in summer the nomad
Pathans, known locally as Kandaris, congregate; so we crossed the Munjan pass
out of Nuristan. We had been warned it was deep in snow, and we engaged four
Nuristanis to help us carry our loads to the top. Near the pass we noticed the
tracks of a leopard. I had already seen three wolves and two bears, and several
times spotted ibex and markhor. Always there seemed to be lammergeyer in the
sky, but only once did I see griffon vultures, circling round a peak. On the whole
we saw few birds in Nuristan.

Below the Munjan pass I met Nicholas Downay, an adventurous young friend
of mine. He had told me in England that he was planning to travel in Nuristan.
Now we sat and talked in a biting wind on the mountainside until our shivering
porters insisted that we went our separate ways.

I followed the Munjan river down to its junction with the Anjuman. Two
Germans had been murdered there the previous year. On a spur above the river
were the ruins of a castle reputedly built by Hulagu, a grandson of Genghis Khan.

cf. p. 250

Still lower down the valley we passed Sar-i-Sang where lapis lazuli was still
mined. All the lapis lazuli so extensively used in ancient Egypt had come from this
one valley in the remote mountains of Central Asia.

The valley widened and we passed cultivated fields and pastures, groves of
poplars, and villages set about with orchards and inhabited by Tajiks and Uzbeks,
who wore turbans, and padded robes of many colours. Roses grew in the hedges.
We came to Jurm, then to the village of Baharak and there we turned aside across
an empty plain towards a rolling sweep of bare mountains. But we were too late.
Down slopes that were almost colourless in the hazy light, but for the vagrant
shadows of scattered clouds, there was winding towards us a continuous thread
of men and camels. They followed no apparent course, turning, twisting, disap-
pearing into hollows, and reappearing. It was already August, and the weather

cf. pp. 258–9, 260–1

had broken. The Kandaris were moving down from Shiva to the plains.

We stood aside to let them pass: camels tied head to tail, laden with tents, poles
and the scanty furnishings and possessions of a nomad people; each camel

decorated with tufted woollen headstalls and wide tasselled neckbands; many with bells fastened above their knees; laden donkeys and horses; small children and a woman or two perched on the loads; women in voluminous clothes with black draperies over their heads, leading strings of camels; bearded men and smooth-faced youths striding past, in turbans, patterned waistcoats and long cloaks; and guard dogs padding by, formidable brutes that could kill a wolf. I had seen the great tribes of northern Arabia, the Bakhtiari of Persia, the Herki of Kurdistan, and the Powindah coming down to Pakistan: yet for some reason, perhaps the landscape, my memory of these Kandaris remains the most vivid of them all.

I went back to Nuristan and from there to Kabul. David Noel, Military Attaché at the British Embassy, drove me in his Land Rover to Mazar-i-Sharif and Herat. Once again I saw the Kandaris, camped now in sheltered valleys, their black tents ranged along the river banks. We would stop the car for a moment, look, and then go on again. Fortunately the projected road on from Mazar-i-Sharif to Herat had then not yet been built. Each evening we camped beside the track, and I stayed awake and listened to the camel bells as the caravans made their way down this cf. pp. 262, 263 immemorial route. We passed Balkh, Mother of Cities, a grave-mound of the past, its monument a crumbling dome and ruined minarets, still of a beauty beyond cf. p. 264 belief. We visited the great mosque in Herat, its spacious court tranquil and impressive. I noticed no other car in Herat. Then the bus arrived and I left for Meshed in Persia. It was October 1965.

I would gladly have gone back another year to Mazar-i-Sharif and done that journey on foot, but the opportunity has passed. Now that the main road is built, the lorries thunder by; the camel caravans are gone, their bells stilled for ever.

OVERLEAF] Northern Pakistan, September 1952, the approach to Chitral from Swat: near the top of the 16,000 ft Kachi Kuni pass. *cf. pages 217–18*

RIGHT] A Chitrali with a double-stringed bow: these shot
not arrows but stones, and were used
in Chitral and over the Afghan border in Nuristan. *cf. page 218*

BELOW] My party on the Baroghil pass. *cf. page 219*

A Kirghiz boy, near the Baroghil pass,
in the far north of Chitral, September 1952.
cf. page 219

Kirghiz from Central Asia, riding over on yaks into northern Kashmir:
near the shrine of Babaghundi, Hunza, September 1953. *cf. page 221*

RIGHT] Rakaposhi, 25,550 ft, the great mountain which dominates
the valley route from Gilgit to Baltit, in Hunza. *cf. page 220*

ABOVE] The 17,000 ft Chilinji pass, on my route from Hunza into Ishkoman. *cf. pages 221–2*

LEFT] A hunter in Ishkoman, a small state adjacent to Hunza, October 1953. *cf. page 223*

FAR LEFT] Hazara
children, central
Afghanistan. *cf. pages 224–7*

RIGHT] A Hazara
tribesman, central
Afghanistan, 1954.
In the days of
British India some of
these tribesmen joined
the Indian Army,
whose intelligence map
and handbook on the
Hazarajat, no proper
survey being possible,
continued well into
this century to be
based exclusively on
their reports. *cf. pages 224–7*

Afghanistan, 1954: a tribesman on the
north-eastern fringe of Hazarajat. *cf. pages 224–7*

BELOW LEFT] A Hazara boy,
near Unai Kotal,
August 1954. *cf. pages 224–7*

BELOW] An Uzbek: visiting the Hazarajat from one of the
Uzbek villages on the borders of the region. *cf. pages 224–7*

LEFT] A Pathan smoking a water-pipe
in a tea-house: North West
Frontier Province of Pakistan, 1952.
cf. pages 226–7

A Powindah on the Pakistani-Afghan border, 1952:
these nomad Pathans were known in different
regions by different names, here as *Powindah*.
cf. pages 226–7

ABOVE RIGHT] A Wazir tribesman near Razmak,
North West Frontier Province of Pakistan, 1952.
cf. page 227

BELOW RIGHT] A Mahsud, near Wana,
North West Frontier Province.
cf. page 227

Nuristan,
north-eastern
Afghanistan,
1956 and 1965:
on the Chamar
pass leading
from the
Panjshir
valley into
Nuristan.
Here at 16,000 ft
we found the
rare snow
formation called
névés pénitents.
cf. page 230

Valley in the Pashaie country. *cf. page 230*

PREVIOUS PAGE] Above the junction of the Kantiwar and Parun valleys, near the village of Mum. The mountain ridges of Nuristan are part of the Hindu Kush. *cf. page 231*

Sari-i-Sang, in Munjan, just north of Nuristan: lapis lazuli mines, sole source of the stone for the ancient world, are here. *cf. page 232*

A typical village in the Minjigal valley, Nuristan. *cf. page 231*

ABOVE]
A boy in the
Kulam valley.
cf. page 230

LEFT]
A Nuristani,
at Puchal in the
Ramgul valley, 1956.
cf. page 230

RIGHT]
An old Nuristani,
up the Parun valley
above Mum, 1965.
cf. page 231

FAR RIGHT]
My Pathan porters
of the Safi tribe,
whom I recruited in
Kamdesh, Nuristan,
1965. *cf. pages 231–2*

A track built up the
cliff, beside a gorge in the
Minjigal valley. *cf. page 231*

RIGHT] A cantilever bridge,
in the Kamdesh valley,
Nuristan. *cf. pages 231–2*

LEFT] Another village
in the Minjigal valley of
Nuristan. *cf. page 231*

ABOVE LEFT]
An example of superb wood carving on the face of a house at Burg-i-Matral, in the Kamdesh valley. *cf. pages 231–2*

BELOW LEFT]
Carved wooden decoration on a village house, perhaps the best of its kind I saw in Nuristan. *cf. pages 231–2*

ABOVE]
A typical carved wooden ornament, set up beside a coffin left in the open, in the Waigul valley. *cf. page 232*

ABOVE RIGHT]
A grave, actually an exposed coffin, in the Waigul valley. *cf. page 232*

BELOW RIGHT]
Horns of markhor, wild goat, flanking an ornamented door: Waigul valley, Nuristan. *cf. page 232*

257

PREVIOUS PAGE]
Badakhshan,
extreme north-
east of
Afghanistan,
August 1965:
Kandari nomads
winding down
towards the
plains from
their summer
camp near
Shiva lake
above the
Oxus valley.
cf. pages 232–3

Kandaris on
the move.
The nomad
Pathans,
known by
various names,
were called
Kandaris
in northern
Afghanistan.
cf. pages 232–3

RIGHT] Detail from an outside wall of the mosque at Balkh. The city, razed in 1221 by Genghis Khan, flowered again under the dynasty of Timur-leng: this lovely blue-domed mosque, built in 1460, now in decay, is an eloquent relic of the Timurids. *cf. page 233*

The mosque at Balkh, northern Afghanistan, 1965. Balkh, now dwindled to a village, was a city of immense antiquity, sited at the junction of immemorial caravan routes, the capital of ancient Bactria, already old when Alexander came. *cf. page 233*

Herat, western Afghanistan, 1965: the Friday Mosque,
a 15th-century rebuilding of a much older fabric.
The great bronze cauldron is dated 1375.
Timur-leng swept over Persia a few years later,
and his son made Herat its capital. *cf. page 233*

THE YEMEN

The Yemen (now the Yemen Arab Republic)

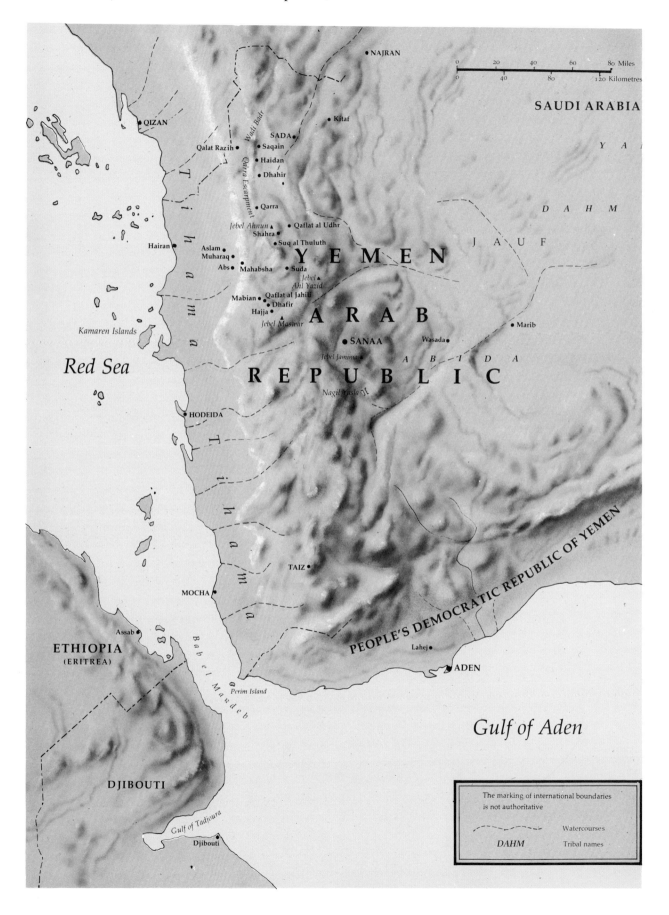

NAJRAN

SAUDI ARABIA

Y A

QIZAN

Wadi Badr

Kitaf

SADA
Saqain
Qalat Razih
Haidan
Dhahir

Qara Escarpment

Qarra

D A H M

Jebel Ahnun ▲ Qaflat al Udhr
Shahra
Suq al Thuluth

J A U F

Hairan

Y E M E N

Aslam
Muharaq
Abs Mahabsha
Suda
Jebel Ahl Yazid ▲

A R A B

Mabian
Dhafir
Qaflat al Jahili
Hajja

Jebel Maswar

Marib

Kamaren Islands

SANAA
Wasada

Red Sea

Jebel Jamima

A B I D A

R E P U B L I C

Nagil Yasla

HODEIDA

T i h a m a

TAIZ

PEOPLE'S DEMOCRATIC REPUBLIC OF YEMEN

MOCHA

Assab

Lahej

Babel Mandeb

ETHIOPIA
(ERITREA)

ADEN

Perim Island

Gulf of Aden

DJIBOUTI

Gulf of Tadjoura

Djibouti

Scale				
0	20	40	60	80 Miles
0	40	80		120 Kilometres

The marking of international boundaries
is not authoritative

– ‧ – ‧ –   Watercourses

DAHM   Tribal names

The Yemen 1966–68

During my years in the Desert, the Yemen had for me the fascination of hostile and forbidden territory, its tribes constantly at war with the Rashid and other tribes among whom I lived. For years I had wanted to travel in that distinctive mountainous country in the south-west of Arabia. Many parts of northern Yemen had been seen by few if any Europeans before the Civil War which broke out in 1962. It was the Civil War which gave me my opportunity to go there in 1966.

To the north the Yemen bordered on Saudi Arabia, to the south on the Aden Protectorate, and to the east, beyond the Jauf and the territories of the Dahm and Abida, it merged into the Empty Quarter. It was in this corner of Arabia that the true Arabs, the sons of Qahtan, were reputed to have originated, distinguished even today from the northern Arabs or the sons of Ishmael; and it was here that the earliest Arabian civilisations, based on the incense trade, took root.

Three or even four thousand years ago the Minaeans, centred on the Jauf, traded as far afield as Petra, Damascus and Egypt, spreading the worship of their Moon God north to the island of Delos in the Mediterranean. Later, throughout the first century BC, the Sabaeans flourished and built the famous dam at Marib, their capital. Strabo wrote, 'From their traffickings the Sabaeans have become the richest of them all, and they have vast equipment of both gold and silver articles, such as couches, tripods and bowls, and very costly houses'. South of Saba, near the valley of the Hadhramaut, was the kingdom of the Himyarites, who rose to power in the second century BC. It was during Himyaritic times that Aelius Gallus, Prefect of Egypt under Augustus, invaded Arabia Felix, resolved to occupy the fabled land of incense. He nearly reached Marib before he was forced to retreat. Gradually the prosperity of this region declined. Arab historians attribute this to the bursting of the great dam at Marib about AD 550, but important factors were the diversion of trade from the overland to the sea route, and invasion by the northern Abyssinians from Axum in AD 525.

Whatever the cause, the inhabitants of the area dispersed, many going as far as Oman, and their palaces became ruins, blown over with sand. With the establishment of Islam the importance of the south declined still further, and the centre of Arab power shifted north to Mecca. Although the Yemenis were converted to Islam there were many revolts against the authority of the Caliph, and in 893 the Zeidi Imam founded a dynasty of king-priests that was still surviving when I arrived in 1966. The Zeidi doctrine, a moderate branch of the Shia belief, prevailed in the north, whereas the orthodox Shafei rite was followed in the coastal plain and the country south of Sanaa.

The Turks occupied the coast in 1849 and the entire country in 1872, but there were frequent insurrections against their oppressive rule. In 1904 the Imam Yahya succeeded his father. From his impregnable stronghold at Shahra on Jebel Ahnun, and at the head of a hundred and fifty thousand northern tribesmen, he fought against the Turks until they granted him recognition. The Turks evacuated the Yemen after defeat in the First World War. The Imam Yahya was murdered in 1948 at the age of eighty and succeeded by his tyrannical son, Ahmed. Surprisingly, Ahmed died peacefully in his bed, succeeded by his son Badr, in 1962. Badr was anxious to modernise and reform the country, but within a week was overthrown by a military coup organised by his trusted friend Abdullah Sallal, supported by President Nasser of Egypt. Sallal proclaimed a Republic. Badr, however, had escaped from the the ruins of his palace in Sanaa, and now rallied most of the northern tribes to his support. These formidable Zeidi tribes would quickly have overcome the less warlike Shafei of the south who, being of a different religious persuasion, supported the Revolution, had not Nasser poured in troops. Armed with tanks, armoured cars, artillery and aircraft, and numbering at least fifty thousand regulars, the Egyptians overran all but a small part of the country. The Royalists were supported by King Faisal of Saudi Arabia, who supplied money and arms, but they never possessed any weapons more formidable than rifles, machine-guns and a few mortars and recoilless guns. Nonetheless, by May 1966 they had driven the Egyptians out of nearly all the north and east of the Yemen, and had detachments in the hills above Sanaa.

My sympathies, naturally, were entirely with the Royalists, and in June 1966, at the invitation of the Royalist Government, I visited Prince Hasan bin Hasan, a cousin of the Imam Badr, at his headquarters at Qarra in north-western Yemen. Badr was now in Taif in Saudi Arabia, his health broken by the hardships of the campaign, and Prince Hasan was acting as Commander-in-Chief in the north. When I arrived at Qarra the tribes who had previously come to terms with the Egyptians were making their submission. Wearing their traditional garb, many of them were dancing the tribal war dance before their Prince to the quick beat of drums, while others were gathered beneath the red flags of the Imamate. Behind were the shallow caves in which the Prince and his retainers lived. Negotiations were going on between Royalists and Republicans and there was a nominal truce, broken however by almost daily bombing and strafing of towns and villages by Egyptian aircraft, and by intermittent skirmishing on the ground. Few of the caves at Qarra would have withstood a direct hit by a heavy bomb, and all would have been death traps if the Egyptians has used gas, as they were doing elsewhere.

The Prince was about thirty years old and spoke good English. Intelligent and well-informed, he worked far into the night, despite poor health, hearing petitions and judging cases. Among his staff were two British wireless operators, also a strange character called Bruce Condé, who had accompanied me to Qarra from Qizan, on the Red Sea near the border between Saudi Arabia and the Yemen. American by birth, with an extraordinary craving for self-aggrandisement, he had assumed the title of Major-General Prince Bourbon Condé, and the designation of Postmaster-General in the Royalist Government.

I had expected to be restricted in my travels, and was delighted when Prince Hasan assured me he would be only too pleased for me to see as much as I wished of the country under his control. The United States and most of Europe had recognised the Republican Government, whereas the British still recognised the Royalists. This was very largely due to Colonel Neil McLean. Since the beginning of the war he had spent months in the Yemen with the Royalists, and as MP for Inverness till 1964 had successfully championed their cause in Parliament. He had encouraged me to visit the Yemen and had put me in touch with the Royalist leaders. I soon realised that I was being accorded a semi-official status to which I had no claim, but this had its uses.

From Qizan I had travelled as far as the foot of the Qarra escarpment in a convoy of lorries and a stink of petrol fumes, but from there I had climbed up into another world. The Prince sent me, together with a *Sayid* as his representative and an escort of five men and two mules, to Shahra, the fortress town on Jebel Ahnun, *cf. pp. 277, 278* from which the Imam Yahya had successfully defied the Turks.

cf. pp. 277, 278

This three-day journey to Shahra was typical of later journeys. Nowhere have I experienced more strenuous travelling than in the Yemen; we would scramble down thousands of feet into a narrow valley, labour up the far side, then down and up again across another gorge, with yet more beyond. Often in the evening I would see our next day's destination apparently only four or five miles away across the plateau, and yet it would take all day to reach it. The lower slopes of Jebel Ahnun were terraced for cultivation but only a single, narrow track gave access to the town of Shahra, placed like a coronet on the mountain-top. The massive houses, four and five storeys high, were built on the very edge of the precipice: from their windows the cliff dropped away for a thousand feet in a sheer fall. In the centre of the town a large cistern collected such rain as fell, and children bathed there throughout the day. The cisterns in all these towns were infected with guinea-worm and many of the townsfolk suffered from it: they wound the worms out of their shins round matchsticks, taking days to extract them. As there was no other drinking water I was lucky to escape infection.

Many houses in Shahra had been damaged by bombing, yet so solidly built *cf. p. 279* were they that sometimes half a house had been sliced off, but the rest was left inhabitable. A few days before we arrived the mosque had been machine-gunned at the time of the midday prayer, and seven people killed, but Shahra was little damaged compared with many towns I later saw. I remained there for a day. After a large and excellent lunch of roast chicken, boiled mutton, soup, rice and various side-dishes, everyone in the hall settled down to chew *qat*, each man with his bundle of fresh-cut twigs before him and a large wad of masticated leaves pouched in his cheek. They sat there, chewing away, until late in the night. This plant (*Catha edulis*) grows wild in the forests of East Africa as a small tree, whereas in the Yemen it is widely cultivated as a bush, and acts as a stimulant. Throughout the Yemen, everyone who could afford it chewed *qat* after lunch. During these sessions I generally went out and wandered round the town, deserted except for *cf. p. 281* children; at this hour they were better company than their elders.

cf. p. 279

cf. p. 281

Despite a haze that never lifted, the view from Shahra over this rock-girt, treeless land was breathtaking, especially when the sun went down behind the mountains and the darkening chasms. And yet this view was not exceptional; during the coming months I was to see scores, all different, but all comparable in grandeur.

We descended the mountain and stayed in the magnificent castle of Qaflat al Udhr, among the Udhr. The Imam Ahmed, Badr's father, had beheaded the son and the brother of Abdullah al Ahmar, the powerful chief of the Hashid confederacy, and in revenge Abdullah now supported the Republicans. Some of the Hashid, however, including the Udhr, were Royalist. I had met some Udhr at Qarra and liked them. In the Yemen I was always on the move and never had the opportunity to know any particular tribe, but I would gladly have stayed a while with them at Qaflat al Udhr. Their turbans and in some cases their clothes were dyed with indigo, which gave them a distinctive and arresting appearance, enhanced by the bandoliers with which they were draped and the large curved daggers they wore. Even young boys carried rifles.

cf. p. 280

From Qaflat we went round the mountain to Suq al Thuluth, the Tuesday market, where we spent an agreeable evening in a crowded caravanserai. Soon after dawn villagers started to arrive and unload their camels, mules and donkeys. At this market Royalist and Republican tribesmen haggled together round stone-built booths under two enormous fig trees. Despite the war and the fact that the Princes who governed these areas spent so much time at interminable conferences outside the Yemen, the everyday life of the countryside went on, and villagers could take their produce to market without fear of pillage. Yet almost every morning we saw aircraft and heard the sound of bombing, as we passed southward along the top of the escarpment.

We stayed in one shattered town after another, and I watched men and boys dancing in triumph amid the ruins of their houses, celebrating the expulsion of the invader whom they hated and despised. The *Sayid* sent word ahead that the Englishman was coming, and the Governor of the town would come out to meet

cf. pp. 284, 285

me, and I would be greeted with a war dance and volleys of rifle-fire. A long column of warriors would escort me to the town; ahead of us three or four boys would dance, their drawn daggers weaving round their heads; behind them came the drummers. Then town dignitaries and even schoolboys would make speeches of welcome. One small round-eyed boy asked me shyly, 'Are you Winston Churchill?' I was sorry to have to disappoint him.

I enjoyed it all enormously but it nearly ended prematurely at Mahabsha. I had been invited to inspect a captured anti-aircraft gun. Accompanied by a large crowd I climbed a steep hill, chatting on the way to two friendly young men from a neighbouring town. We reached the gun and they urged me to take photographs. Since the barrel was pointing at me I moved a pace or two aside to get a better angle, and they stepped into my place as I did so. I noticed that someone was sitting in the gunner's seat. The next moment the gun fired straight at us. Both my companions were killed; my clothes were spattered with their blood.

There was instantly chaos. The kinsmen of the dead men tried to kill the gunner; others tried to defend him. Someone in authority intervened and the gunner was escorted to the town; he had fired by mistake while trying to elevate the barrel, and the case was settled that evening with blood money.

From Mahabsha we descended the escarpment by a long, steep track to Muharaq, where I spent the next day at the crowded weekly market. I was back in the Tihama, a world similar to the one I had known and enjoyed in the Hejaz twenty years before. The people, darker and quite distinct from the mountain Arabs, had refined gentle faces and easy informal manners. Their clothes, too, were different: short white loincloths, tight-sleeved jackets, large straw hats and plaited conical skull-caps. They lived in wattle and daub huts. Each night they danced to the quick staccato beat of their drums. Until recently the Egyptians had occupied these villages; they were still only a few miles away at Abs.

We climbed back up the escarpment to Mahabsha and went south as far as Jebel ahl Yazid, within a day's march of Sanaa, still held by the Egyptians. We marched long hours, as many as ten and twelve a day. The drought had broken and dark rainstorms drove across the parched land. One especially spectacular storm raged over the fifteen thousand foot Jebel Maswar; sometimes they missed us, sometimes they burst upon us. Everywhere along our route towns and villages lay in ruins. We stopped at Suda, with not a house undamaged; at Dhafir, where only the three tombs of the Imams had miraculously escaped; and Mabian, where the town and the famous mosque had been pounded to rubble; the inhabitants sheltered in caves below the town, and died later when the Egyptians used gas. I carried a box of medicines and did what I could for the sick and wounded. Several times I was taken forward to view the Egyptian positions, and would gladly have dispensed with the crowd that followed me.

cf. pp. 280, 282, 283

I returned to Qarra where I had to wait a month till Prince Hasan returned from Saudi Arabia. Then, escorted by one of his guards and with a boy and two donkeys, I went north along the escarpment. We stayed two days at Dhahir, where tribesmen from the surrounding villages and from the coastal plain crowded the streets for the weekly market. Here local boys, as old as sixteen, wore their hair cut like haloes round their heads; while others, from the lowlands, had a broad strip shaved through their hair from ear to ear. Both styles indicated that they were still uncircumcised.

cf. p. 280

We stayed again in Haidan where after dark men and boys danced and drummed late into the night under a full moon. A small colony of Yemeni Jews lived here, gentle inoffensive people, distinguished by their ringlets.

We came to Saqain where seven-storeyed houses were built of mud and resembled the *kasbahs* of the High Atlas; but the centre of the town had been bombed to ruins. Next day we followed the Wadi Badr, where the tribesmen had taken a bloody vengeance, ambushing and destroying a large column of Egyptians; anyone who tried to escape had been hunted down and killed. I had become accustomed to burnt-out tanks, armoured cars and lorries. There were many here. At nearby Qalat Razih the walls still bore evidence of where the defenders had been wiped out; young men pointed with pride to the faded blood-stains where they had killed.

cf. pp. 288–9

cf. pp. 286–7

We turned eastward, skirted Sada, still held by the Egyptians, and came to Kitaf, where Prince Hasan bin Yahya, Prime Minister and father of Prince Hasan with whom I had stayed at Qarra, had his headquarters. An elderly man, uninfluenced by personal ambition, he was a dedicated Royalist. He had assumed the Imamate when news arrived of Badr's death in the rising in Sanaa, but immediately relinquished it on hearing that Badr was alive after all. I liked him best of all the Yemeni Princes.

The Egyptians bombed Kitaf fairly regularly at eight in the morning, so everyone always left the town before the bombers arrived, to shelter in the nearby lava fields. One morning on my way there I came under fire from machine-guns and rifles, and dived for cover. I thought we had been surprised by the Republicans, until I noticed the hare at which the Royalist army were shooting. Three months later nine aircraft with poison gas bombed Kitaf: several hundred people and all the animals in the area were killed.

cf. p. 292

From Kitaf I visited Najran just across the Saudi border. The town, unrecognisably enlarged since 1947, was the main base for the forthcoming offensive in the eastern Yemen. From there on my way to the front at Sanaa, I was given a lift as far as Hairan in a lorry carrying arms and ammunition. Convoys travelled by night but were attacked by aircraft using flares. We spent a day in the Jauf among the Dahm. They had been our bitter enemies when I travelled with the Rashid in the Sands. Now I was happy to be among them, for they were Bedu; even their voices reminded me of those bygone days. On a later occasion I stayed in their tents and there I met men who had known Musallim bin al Kamam and who spoke of bin Duailan, 'The Cat', who had died not far from there in his last great fight against the Yam. 'Are you the Christian who travelled with the Rashid? Welcome! Hey, boy, hurry and milk the red one. Hurry!' It was all so familiar; lawless as ever, the Dahm looted arms from Royalist convoys when chance offered, but I knew that while I was with them I was safe. I never felt as confident with the highland tribes, among whom treachery was not unknown. The Republicans offered large rewards for Europeans serving the Royalists.

I spent a month in the country round Sanaa, travelling on foot from one Royalist position to another. I looked across the stony, sun-scorched plain from Jebel Jamima to Sanaa, the Royalist goal, now tantalisingly close after four years of war. During those days I stayed with various Princes and tribal leaders, sharing their cheerless quarters in caves among the hills. In November 1966, after five months in the Yemen, I went back to England. There I had the cartilages removed from both knees; apparently I had worn them out.

While I was in England Egypt suffered an overwhelming defeat by Israel in the Six Days War, and in consequence Nasser withdrew all his troops from the Yemen. I went back there in November 1967 and arrived at the headquarters near Sanaa of Prince Muhammad al Hussain, Commander-in-Chief on the southern front. With him I found my old friend, Colonel Neil McLean, and Mark Lennox-Boyd. Prince Hussain's camp was dispersed among the barren rocky hills and there was a constant coming and going of tribesmen affirming their allegiance, and of camels and donkeys bringing supplies from Wasada at the foot of the eastern escarpment. It resembled settings and scenes from *Seven Pillars of Wisdom*.

In the morning four days later the camp was attacked by aircraft that bombed, rocketed and machine-gunned the area. Hearing the planes, McLean, Lennox-Boyd and I had taken shelter in a shallow watercourse. I was watching the first Mig sweep low down the valley when it opened fire. A shell burst on a nearby rock and a splinter nicked my head. I dropped further into cover. A little later I heard McLean say in an irritated voice, 'Damn it, look what you've done, Wilfred.' Blood from my head had soaked the box of cigars he had brought with him for safe-keeping.

The attacks continued into the afternoon. Four people were killed and twelve badly wounded. These included the prince's coffee-boy, a child of perhaps thirteen; his foot was almost blown off. I could have removed it and done something for the others if my box of medicines had not been abandoned in a cave on the way here, owing to lack of transport. The wounded were lifted into a lorry and laid on the bare boards for a nightmare journey to Najran; not one of them made a sound.

Two days later the Royalists shot down a Mig and we went to look at the wreckage. The pilot was an unidentifiable mess, but his map and various notes were in Russian. The Egyptians had gone but the Russians had arrived.

cf. p. 293 The Prince moved closer to Sanaa and established himself in a large cave. McLean, Lennox-Boyd and I were handicapped throughout because we had no transport, no servant and no provisions, and I was not yet fully mobile after my operations. It was very cold at night. We each carried a couple of blankets and fed and slept where we could. We ate with the Prince if we were in time for a meal; his cave was always packed with retainers and it was hard to find anywhere to stretch out at night. I often went forward to join the French mercenaries where they were mortaring the camps round Sanaa with their 4-inch mortar. They were congenial and being French fed well. Above all, there was room for me to sleep in their tent, which they had dug down for protection from the shelling. Snug after dark, they would roar out the marching songs of the Legion, while mortar bombs exploded around them in the valley. The Royalists frequently attacked at night, and then flare after flare went up from the Republican lines; the flash of guns and the arching tracer flickered along the horizon. Time and again the tribesmen would capture a position, only maddeningly to abandon it and go off with their loot.

cf. pp. 290–1

McLean and I visited the pass at Nagil Yasla two days after the battle in which Prince Hasan Ismail, yet another of the Princes, had managed to throw back a large force from Taiz attempting to open the road to Sanaa. He had done this although the Republicans had artillery and tanks, whereas the Royalists were armed only with rifles, machine-guns and a single 4-inch mortar. The villagers had turned on the fleeing Republicans and hunted them down: the mountainside and plain below were littered with corpses, many stripped of their clothes; each of these had been left with a tuft of herbs between its legs for the sake of decency.

cf. p. 292

I had feared Sanaa would fall before I got there. Now it looked as if this inconclusive siege would go on indefinitely. It had all been an interesting experience but I could not stay there for ever. I had plans to travel in northern Kenya, and in January 1968 I returned to England. In fact the Royalists never captured Sanaa, and a compromise government was eventually established in the Yemen.

cf. pp. 294, 295

During his long reign the Imam Yahya administered his people in accordance with the Sharia, that strict Islamic code which governed every aspect of their lives. His brutal son Ahmed was hated by many; the intermittent rebellions were directed at him personally, not at the code by which he ruled; indeed all but a handful of his subjects would have considered any concession to Western innovations anathema. Only a few revolutionaries, educated abroad, regarded the Government as archaic. Badr, during his father's lifetime, had sympathised with some of the revolutionaries and intervened on their behalf. It was ironic that these very people, supported by the Shafei tribes of the south on religious grounds, drove him from his capital, and that it was reactionary northern tribesmen who rallied to support him. They fought and many died on his behalf, but with the final establishment of a Republic a dynasty which had endured a thousand years, and was still approved by the majority of Yemenis, came to an end.

The fortress town of Shahra, on the crest of Jebel Ahnun, northern Yemen:
the foreground shows the intensive cultivation of the mountainside. *cf. page 271*

The westward view from the Imam's Palace, Shahra.
From this impregnable base an earlier Imam
had for years successfully defied the Turks. *cf. page 271*

RIGHT] Shahra: the result of Egyptian bombing
of the massive houses of the town, 1966. *cf. page 271*

LEFT] A group of Yemeni children in their village, badly damaged by Egyptian air attacks, 1966. The bomb round which they were clustered had not exploded, and was dangerous. *cf. page 273*

ABOVE RIGHT] Udhr tribesmen, at Qaflat al Udhr, 1966: unlike others of the Hashid confederacy the Udhr were Royalist in the Yemen Civil War. *cf. pages 271–2*

ABOVE] A fourteen-year-old of the Udhr tribe serving with Prince Hasan bin Hasan's forces at Qaflat al Udhr. Many boys even younger than this one were fighting in the Royalist ranks, 1966. *cf. pages 271–2*

BELOW RIGHT] A Bani Huruth tribesman at Dhahir on the edge of the escarpment, northern Yemen, 1966. *cf. page 273*

RIGHT]
The Yemen,
1966:
a young man
smoking a
water-pipe.
cf. pages 269–275

LEFT]
Qaflat al Jahili,
after it had
been bombed
by the Egyptians.
cf. page 273

RIGHT]
The town of Suda,
northern Yemen,
likewise heavily
damaged by
Egyptian bombing,
1966.
cf. page 273

Part of the Royalist army at Mahabsha. Boys dancing
with drawn daggers led them, followed by the drummers. *cf. page 272*

RIGHT] Tribesmen, who had earlier come out to welcome me, dancing
their war dance at Mahabsha, on the edge of the escarpment. *cf. page 272*

BELOW] The war dance. *cf. page 272*

Saqain, in northern Yemen. *cf. page 273*

PREVIOUS PAGE] A group of boys at Qalat Razih, soon after its recapture by the Royalists. *cf. page 273*

A 4-inch mortar, with which in late 1967 French mercenaries in the Royalist positions
investing Sanaa bombarded the Republican camps around the city. *cf. page 275*

Kitaf, headquarters of the Yemeni Royalist Prime Minister,
Prince Hasan bin Yahya, being bombed by Egyptian aircraft in 1966.
cf. page 273

RIGHT] In this cave, in late 1967, Prince Muhammad al Hussain,
Royalist Commander-in-Chief on the southern front, established his
headquarters for what was to be the final assault on the capital, Sanaa.
cf. page 274

BELOW] Corpses of Yemeni Republican troops after the battle at Nagil Yasla,
1967: the Royalists had repulsed a much superior force, inflicting heavy losses.
cf. page 275

Sanaa, capital of the Yemen:
the military goal which the
Royalists failed to attain.
These two photographs were
taken in 1977, years after the
Civil War was over. *cf. pages 274–5, 296*

Epilogue 1977–78

In 1977 I returned briefly to Arabia. First I went to the Yemen as the guest of Hugh Leach, and stayed in Sanaa, which previously I had seen only from afar with the Royalist forces. Yemeni labourers, working in Saudi Arabia, were now remitting to their families the equivalent of half a million pounds a day, and the disruptive effect of this undreamed wealth was everywhere apparent. I travelled for a week on foot among the villages in the Tihama; but even there the contentment I had formerly found was now largely gone. The tribesmen grumbled that their needs were being neglected or that a neighbouring community had received more aid than they had. Taiz, unfortunately, had been demolished and rebuilt, but the old walled city of Sanaa had so far escaped redevelopment, though in its narrow streets motor-cycles had taken the place of donkeys, and television masts were on every building. The streets in the adjacent New Town were frequently jammed by traffic. Everything was changing fast.

Next I went to Oman, as the guest of the Government. Helicopters, aeroplanes, cars and launches were put at my disposal. I was flown to Salala, once a straggling Arab village, now a town with traffic lights. From there Musallim bin Tafl and the Bait Kathir sheikhs took me, escorted by many cars, along sign-posted roads to the new town on top of Jebel Qarra, where they drove me out to see the airport, then entertained me in their concrete houses. When I had come to Dhaufar in 1945, Bertram Thomas was the only European who had crossed this range.

Next day I flew in a helicopter to bin Kabina's tents in the desert. There he and bin Ghabaisha met me, grey-bearded now, twenty-seven years since our parting in Dubai. Bin Kabina had slaughtered a camel for the feast. As we approached his tent the waiting tribesmen fired over our heads with the automatic rifles that they now possessed. I had known many of these Rashid, though some were hard to recognise. Several of my old friends were dead: their sons pressed forward to greet me. I was moved to be among them once again, but I knew that our old relationship was irrevocably gone.

Then, accompanied by bin Kabina and bin Ghabaisha, I flew to Muscat. Till recently it had been a fine old Arab seaport. The late Sultan, Sayid Said bin Timur, had feared the effect of Western materialism on his people; insofar as he was able he had banned the entry of modern innovations; no car, for instance, could be imported without his express permission. In the end he had been deposed by his son Qabus, who opened the flood-gates. Modern houses, office blocks and hotels now stretched along the motorway up the coast, far beyond Matrah.

We went by car to Nazwa where the aged Imam had ruled Inner Oman from his impregnable fort, striving with the support of his subjects to maintain the ancient values. He had been overthrown by his inveterate enemy the late Sultan, with the assistance of the British, and now Qabus was modernising Inner Oman, building roads and schools and hospitals. At Nazwa a concrete mosque of alien design, comparable in size to the fort, was being built alongside it; the visual effect was disastrous. We climbed Jebel al Akhadar. The Sultan had offered to fly me to the top in a helicopter, and bin Kabina and bin Ghabaisha could not understand why I preferred to go on foot, a last gesture to the past. There was an army camp on the mountain where aeroplanes and helicopters landed and took off.

But my visit to Abu Dhabi was the most traumatic experience of my return to Arabia. Thirty years earlier I had waded the creek and ridden across open desert to the Sheikh's fort. Now a modern city covered the entire island and extended on to the mainland, where a dual carriageway across the Sands linked it with a new town at Muwaiqih called Al Ain. When oil was discovered in this territory Sheikh Shakhbut had spent very little of the vast amount of money he received; he was reputed to keep it in a box stowed under his bed. He feared with every reason the effect that it would have upon his people, perhaps twelve thousand in all. Another discerning ruler vainly trying to stem the tide, he had been condemned, especially by the British officials, as mean, obstructive, unrealistic and old-fashioned, and been replaced as ruler by his brother Zayid. Unembittered, Shakhbut now lived in Muwaiqih, a wise, courteous old man with a quick, enquiring mind. Meanwhile the Bedu, who had once herded their animals in the desert during the winter and dived for pearls in summer, now received everything from the Government: large subsidies for their livestock; free medicine; free schooling, with a cash bonus for attendance; free housing. Everything indeed was provided; there was no longer need to strive for anything – immigrants were pouring in to do the work.

All that is best in the Arabs came from the desert. Scholars argue that Islam was a product of the town. Certainly Muhammad was a townsman and a merchant, but Mecca and Medina were small, isolated desert towns, and Muhammad's frequent journeyings were with camels through the wilderness. Desert Arabs had implicit belief in the existence of God and it was this that found fulfilment in Islam; they also had a sense of fellowship which helped to bind them, members of one faith. From the desert too has come the Arabs' pride of race, their generosity and sense of hospitality; their dignity and the regard they have for the dignity of others; their humour, their courage and their patience; the language that they speak, and their passionate love of poetry. But they are a race who produce their best only under conditions of extreme hardship. Lawrence described the nomad life as the circulation which kept vigour in the Semitic body and wrote, 'There were few, if indeed there was a single northern Semitic, whose ancestors had not at some dark age passed through the desert. The mark of nomadism, that most deep and biting social discipline, was on each of them in his degree.'

Significantly, it was the desert Arabs who impressed their characteristics on the Arab race, and not the more numerous inhabitants of the Yemen, with their tradition of an ancient civilisation. It was the customs and standards of the desert which had been accepted by townsmen and villagers alike, and which had been spread by the Arab conquests across North Africa and the Middle East, and by Islam across a great part of the world. The desert Arabs had no tradition of civilisation behind them; no architectural inheritance – they lived in black tents, or in rooms devoid of furnishings in their villages and towns. They had no taste for refinements, demanded only the bare necessities of life. It was a life that produced much that was noble, little that was gracious and nothing that was artistic.

These desert Arabs were avaricious, rapacious and predatory, born freebooters, contemptuous of all outsiders, and intolerant of restraint. In the seventh century, united for the first and probably the last time in their history, they swept out of Arabia and carried all before them. In little over a century their rule extended from the Pyrenees and the shores of the Atlantic to the Indus and the borderlands of China. They had emerged from the desert craving for plunder and united by a burning faith; it would not have been surprising if they had proved to be another scourge, similar to the hordes of Attila or of Genghis Khan. It is one of the miracles of history that instead they founded a new civilisation, uniting in one society the hitherto incompatible cultures of the Mediterranean and of Persia.

Arabic, evolved as a dialect of nomad herdsmen in the desert, developed into one of the great languages of the world, flexible enough to translate every shade of Greek philosophy and thought and pass it back to the West. As the Muslim faith and Arabic language spread throughout their Empire, the distinction between Arabs and their far more numerous subjects largely disappeared; conquerors and conquered tended to become fellow-Muslims.

The resulting Muslim civilisation was profoundly influenced by Greek thought, but while it assimilated much it was never merely imitative, and it made its own great contribution to the world in architecture, literature, philosophy, history, mathematics, astronomy, physics, chemistry and medicine. Although few of the great intellectual figures of this society were Arabs, and several were not even Muslims but Jews and Christians, it was Arabs who founded and at first ruled this civilisation. Without them neither the Alhambra nor the Taj Mahal would have been built. Today some one hundred and thirty million people speak Arabic as their mother tongue, and a seventh part of the human race profess Islam.

With the discovery and exploitation of oil the life of the Bedu has now disappeared from Arabia, vanished in the course of a decade or two as utterly as the life of the prairie Indian in North America. Bin Kabina and bin Ghabaisha still lived in black tents and owned herds of camels, but they went everwhere in cars and loaded their tents and chattels into lorries when they moved their camps; their sons, who had never known the harsh discipline of the desert, would eventually seek employment in the towns. I remember asking bin Kabina, when we reached Mukalla in 1947, why he did not buy a blanket; I shrank from the thought of him sleeping on the freezing sand, covered only with his loincloth. 'I am a Bedu; cold won't hurt me. I want to save my money to buy camels.' 'I am a Bedu.' That had been their proud boast, their answer to every challenge. 'Bedu' today is a term of abuse shouted by pedestrians at careless drivers. The values of the desert have vanished: all over Arabia the transistor has replaced the tribal bard.

I had returned to Abu Dhabi at the express invitation of my old friend Zayid, but once there I found it difficult to get in touch with him. Eventually his secretary told me that I could meet him at the Agricultural Show at Al Ain. There I watched Arab schoolboys in flared trousers and sequined jackets playing 'pop' music on guitars, while other boys and girls moved in procession, carrying plastic palms. Grey-bearded men watched this betrayal of their culture with evident approval. I was filled with despair. I found it tragic that the Arabs, who have contributed so much to the world, should now so easily be seduced by the tawdriest and most trivial aspects of Western civilisation.

After the Agricultural Show I met Sheikh Zayid in the spurious splendour of the Al Ain Hilton, and remembered with nostalgia our first meeting, thirty years before, when I had couched my camel near here and walked forward to greet him where he sat upon the sand among his Bedu.

cf. p. 111

British travellers in Arabia are often accused of romantic attitudes about the Arabs. This may well be true of some, but rarely of those who over long periods shared the lives and privations of their Arab companions. Burton, Doughty and Philby were never romantic about them in their writings. Lawrence as a young man at Carchemish may have been but certainly was not by the time he reached Damascus. In *Seven Pillars of Wisdom* he wrote, 'Bedouin ways were hard, even for those brought up in them and for strangers terrible: a death in life.' Many will assert that in this case any change must be for the better. I would never accept this. The Arabs whose lives I shared in the Desert, and later in the Marshes, were not just content but happy. My abiding memory is of their cheerfulness and courage. Among them I never met a depressed or neurotic individual. Now that the Arabs are among the economic masters of the world I fear that many will find unendurable the boredom of their wealth.

I have travelled through some of the most magnificent scenery in the world and lived among interesting and little-known tribes, yet no country has moved me as did the deserts of Arabia. No man can live there and emerge unchanged. He will carry, however faint, the imprint of the desert, the brand which marks the nomad; and he will have within him, weak or insistent according to his nature, the yearning to return. For that cruel land can cast a spell no temperate clime can match.

Glossary of some Foreign Terms used in the Text

Agha	(*Persian & Kurdish*) In Kurdistan, a chief.
Ailoq	(*Persian*) Herdsmen's summer pasture camp.
Amir	(*Arabic*) Prince or ruler. (Also *Emir* or *Mir*).
Bimbashi	(*Turkish*) The lowest British commissioned rank in the Sudan Defence Force: originally equivalent to Colonel in the Egyptian Army.
Boom	(*Arabic*) Large type of ocean-going *dhow* (*q.v.*).
Burnous	(*Arabic*) Garment resembling a cloak with a hood.
Caliph	(*Arabic*) Title of Islamic rulers in succession from the Prophet Muhammad. (Also *Khalifa*)
Dejazmatch	(*Amharic*) Title equivalent to senior general.
Dhow	(*Arabic*) Term loosely applied by foreigners to Arab sailing vessels.
Dinar	(*Arabic/Persian* from *late Greek* and *Latin denarius*) A coin roughly comparable with £1 in Iraqi currency.
Doroshkeh	(*Persian* from *Russian*) Horse-drawn cab.
Faqir	(*Arabic*) Term loosely applied to members of ascetic or mendicant orders. (Also *Fakir*)
Gendarme	(*Persian* from *French*) Member of Iranian para-military force.
Ghaf	(*Arabic*) The tree *Prosopsis spicigera L.*
Goum, Goumier	(*French* from *Arabic*) Colonial mounted troops, North Africa.
Hausa	(*Arabic*) Tribal war dance.
Imam	(*Arabic*) Term of widely varying meaning in the Middle East – priest, saint, successor to the Prophet, religious/political ruler.
Jebel	(*Arabic*) Hill, mountain. (Also *Jabal*)
Kasbah	(*Arabic*) A fortress building, North Africa.
Machan	(*Hindustani*) Platform for shooting from, usually in a tree.
Madan	(*Arabic*) Collective name for the Iraqi marsh-dwellers.
Mishqa	(*Arabic*) Among tribes of the Yemen and Saudi Arabia, a general name for the southern (Badhramaut) tribes.
Mudhif	(*Arabic*) A sheikh's reed-built guest house in and around the marshes of southern Iraq.
Muharram	(*Arabic*) An Arabic month, covering the period of mourning for the *Imam* Hussein (died AD 680).
Mullah	(*Arabic*) Variously an Islamic teacher, priest or leader.
Nasrani	(*Arabic*) Nazarene, Christian.
Negus	(*Amharic*) King.
Névés pénitents	(*French*) Rare formation of snow and ice pinnacles bearing some resemblance to cowled monks.
Qaid	(*Arabic*) A distinctive formation of permanent sharp-ridged dunes.
Qasab	(*Arabic*) The tall reed *Phragmites communis*.
Qassis	(*Arabic*) The plant *Cyperus conglomeratus Rottb*.
Qat	(*Arabic*) *Catha edulis*, a tree or shrub with narcotic properties. (Also *Miraa*)
Rabia	(*Arabic*) A tribesman accompanying strangers to guarantee their safety with his own or related tribes. (Also *Rafiq*)
Ramadhan	(*Arabic*) The Islamic month of fasting.
Ras	(*Amharic*) A rank or title often equated with that of Duke.
Safari	(*Swahili* from *Arabic*) Journey, expedition, travel.
Sahib	(*Arabic*) Its Arabic meaning (unlike derived usages in Persia India, etc) is *friend*: as such, a nickname of the author in the Marshes of Iraq.
Salam alaikum	(*Arabic*) Standard greeting, meaning (like the standard reply *Alaikum as salam*) Peace be on you.
Sayid	(*Arabic*) A person having or claiming descent from the Prophet.
Shaitan	(*Arabic*) Satan, the Devil.
Sharia	(*Arabic*) Islamic Law, from the Coran and related texts.
Sheikh	(*Arabic*) Tribal leader.
Shia	(*Arabic*) A major variant from orthodox Islamic doctrine: and its followers.
Sowar	(*Urdu/Persian*) A mounted orderly or trooper.
Sudd	(*Arabic*) Marsh area of the Upper Nile, Sudan.
Sunni	(*Arabic*) The name of the orthodox ('lawful') branch of Islam; and its followers.
Suq	(*Arabic*) A permanent or regular bazaar in a town or village.
Syce	(*Hindustani/Arabic*) A groom. (Also *Sais*)
Tagrud	(*Arabic*) Marching song to which the Bedu trot their camels.
Trek	(*Cape Dutch*) Journey, expedition, *safari*.
Umbarak	(*Arabic*) Literally blessed one, used as an Arabic name: as such, a nickname of the author in Southern Arabia.
Wadi	(*Arabic*) River-bed, watercourse.
Wali	(*Arabic/Turkish*) Local civil Governor.
Yurt	(*Turkish*) A Turkoman nomad's felt tent.
Zahra	(*Arabic*) The yellow-flowering plant *Tribulus spp*.

Index

The italic marginal references in the text are to the relevant page(s) of photographs; similarly the italic references at the end of picture captions are to the relevant passages of text. In this Index of principal Proper Names, some of the more extensive references are show in heavy type; references to illustrations are in italics; references to maps are preceded by the letter M. The Biographical Summary on p. 11 has not been indexed.